GRACE, GUIDANCE, AND GIFTS

GRACE, GUIDANCE, AND GIFTS

Sacred Blessings to Light Your Way

SONIA CHOQUETTE

HAY HOUSE, INC.
Carlsbad, California • New York City
London • Sydney • New Delhi

Published in the United States by: Hay House, Inc.: www.hayhouse
.com® • *Published in Australia by:* Hay House Australia Pty. Ltd.:
www.hayhouse.com.au • *Published in the United Kingdom by:*
Hay House UK, Ltd.: www.hayhouse.co.uk • *Published in India by:*
Hay House Publishers India: www.hayhouse.co.in

Cover design: Julie Davison • *Interior design:* Tricia Breidenthal

The author of this book does not dispense medical advice or
prescribe the use of any technique as a form of treatment for physical,
emotional, or medical problems without the advice of a physician,
either directly or indirectly. The intent of the author is only to offer
information of a general nature to help you in your quest for emotional
and spiritual well-being. In the event you use any of the information
in this book for yourself, the author and the publisher assume no
responsibility for your actions.

Library of Congress Cataloging-in-Publication Data

Choquette, Sonia.
  Grace, guidance, and gifts : sacred blessings to light your way / Sonia
Choquette. -- 1st ed.
     p. cm.
  ISBN 978-1-4019-3744-7 (tradepaper : alk. paper) 1. Spiritual life. 2.
Devotional literature. I. Title.
  BL624.C47686 2012
  204'.4--dc23
                              2012005961

Tradepaper ISBN: 978-1-4019-3744-7
Digital ISBN: 978-1-4019-3745-4

1st edition, July 2012

Printed in the United States of America

To my beloved daughters,
Sonia and Sabrina Choquette Tully.
I love you.

CONTENTS

INTRODUCTION

As Divine Beings we are on a continuing transformational journey from limited human consciousness to limitless Divine Spiritual consciousness, and we have two distinct aspects of self that are in the process of merging: our soul and our Divine Spirit.

Our soul is not the same thing as our Spirit, although for many people, myself included, this has been, at times, an unclear and confusing distinction, because both are aspects of our nonphysical being and are therefore difficult to separate.

Having been asked the difference between Spirit and soul over the years by my clients and students, and having wondered myself, I have set my heart and mind to finding this answer for decades. Now, after years of prayer, meditation, contemplation, discussion, wonder, and intuition, I have come to recognize and understand the distinction between the two in such a way that, at least for me, feels true. Our soul self embodies the sum total of our conscious experiences throughout each lifetime, and we carry this totality of consciousness from one lifetime to the next. Throughout our human journey, our soul seeks to find its way back home, back to Source.

The soul contains all our feelings, involvements, learning, love, confusion, and understanding from our first moment of separation from Source to the present, where we yearn for the moment of reunion. That is why the soul *seeks*. It is on a mission to get back home, back to Source, and it draws from all of its experiences as it works to achieve wholeness.

Our Spirit, on the other hand, is the timeless divine spark of holiness within, the eternal flame of light that has never been separated from Source. An extension of the One Spirit, our Spirit oversees the soul on its journey home. While the soul is the "self" that experiences life, the Spirit is the witness overseeing the "experiencing" part of you that is learning.

Energetically, the vibration of soul and Spirit is quite different. The soul's vibration feels energetically complex, both light and dark, and even in some more than a bit fragmented. The soul energy feels at times cloudy, heavy, and attached, while at other times yearning, restless, intense, and compelled, even shadowy like the moon. The soul is complex because it is composed of so many experiences: positive, beautiful, and transcendent, as well as horrific, traumatic, and painful. It reflects and expresses these complexities through our ego as it seeks the light, and draws from the patterns of the past for guidance and support on its quest. Sometimes this is good. Other times this holds back the soul.

When ruled *solely* by the soul/ego, we tend to repeat old, outworn patterns of behavior, can become clouded by our perceptions, lack clear boundaries, get distracted and confused by others, live sentimentally in the past, allow our ego's fears to outshine love, and lose our true identity. We absorb the negativity and needs of others, and lose a strong connection to our authentic Self in present time. We become easily depressed and angered, and feel victimized. Our eyes are dull, our emotions are heavy, our energy is depleted, and we become passive and overwhelmed.

Introduction

Our Spirit, on the other hand, feels energetically light, buoyant, without edges or limits, like a clear, bright eternal ray; a vibrant, always-present sun. There is no past to one's Spirit. There is no story or experience to carry. There is no darkness to illuminate. There is no timeline to follow, no urgency to seek, no restlessness to overcome. There is only peace, only light. The Spirit within is our God-self being itself. In Spirit there is no "dark night," as with the soul. There is only perfect and ceaseless illuminating light.

When the Spirit within us rules, we have a clear and strong sense of who we are, and we know our boundaries and express them clearly, as well as respect the boundaries of others. We can easily deflect negativity, stand in the waves of strong emotion without losing ourselves, remain grounded and calm under pressure, see the humor in all things, and easily laugh at ourselves and at life's absurdities. We have a bright sparkle in our eyes, an easy smile on our lips, and a bounce in our walk. We live in the moment; are fully aware of our co-creative power; and have energy, enthusiasm, confidence, and love to give, receive, and share.

Our conscious human quest is to merge our soul with our authentic Spirit, to lead our soul home. And the best way to do this is to strengthen the attention and focus we place on our Spirit over that of the soul.

As human beings fascinated with our own history, dramas, false perceptions, and pains, our attention has sadly drifted away from our Divine Timeless Spirit as guide. We have instead become ensconced in using soul perception as our guide. While we are here to grow our soul and learning takes place within the soul, we will not find the light of Spirit and return to Source by strictly following the path of the soul. The way home is the other way around. When we connect to the light of Spirit within and let its brilliant light lead, our soul finds its way back to Source much more quickly.

In keeping our attention and focus on our Spirit, we reeducate the intellect, and guide the soul to fully surrender and follow the light rather than fight and struggle in the darkness. This sounds difficult, because we are used to learning through the lens of the soul, and through that lens, everything feels challenging. I am grateful that with our Spirit in charge, all becomes clear, just like turning on a light in a dark room.

This book and accompanying meditation program (in an audio download) serve to help you unite your soul with your Spirit. Together they are designed to shift your ingrained patterns of focus and behavior away from the limiting perceptions of soul and ego, and toward unlimited surrender to Spirit. Most important, the book and meditations help you open up and receive the three *essential* blessings from our Creator that make possible this shift of vibration from soul to Spirit. These blessings are *grace, guidance,* and *gifts.* Without these blessings, you remain stuck in ego and soul, and continue to suffer. This book and meditations help establish the fundamental and necessary groundwork of daily reminder, intention, acceptance, and activation of these blessings in your life so that you can connect with the Holy Spirit within.

This book and meditation program also reflect the way that I have been personally led to surrender to Spirit over soul in my own life. In this work, I share the same teachings, prayers, and blessings I have received to connect with Spirit throughout my entire life. Through a daily routine of recognizing and accepting my blessings and living more and more in Spirit, I have grown from being just an intuitive guide on the path for others, to actually being a conduit for others by way of embodying and activating the power of Spirit in others directly.

My Personal Journey

Reflecting upon my own personal journey, starting as an intuitive guide when I was a young woman to my present service as an energetic catalyst and direct conduit to Source and Holy Spirit, I can now clearly see that my own internal vibrational energetic frequency has dramatically shifted and expanded through the very practices I have laid out in this book.

I am not the same person I was years ago, on any level: physically, energetically, emotionally, or spiritually. I originally started my spiritual journey at a very young age in order to grow my soul, and I focused very much on it. Along the way, I, like everyone, struggled and fought to ease the pain and restriction of my soul patterns. It was like fighting my way out of a rabbit hole. I kept falling back in, over and over again. I made progress, but it was sloppy and slow.

Today, however, through my constant focus on God's blessings upon me, I am happily no longer struggling as I once did. While I am still aware of my soul patterns and ego filters, and still work on moving them into the light, I am now Spirit centered and mostly filled with an unwavering light, internal joy, peace, and confidence that I never expected or assumed would happen in me as it has. And I am gratefully free of any *major* soul drama. It still comes and goes, as it always will, because I do have a soul and it must continue to grow, but soul drama does not possess and control me as it once did. I feel my soul struggle, but I do not fall unconsciously into victimhood as easily anymore and I don't stay there as long. Instead, I am able to see and dismantle the dramas I face and create, and liberate my soul with the power of my Spirit and the help of the grace, guidance, and gifts I've received from God.

In retrospect, I admit that this was not necessarily the result of a purposeful transformational plan on my part, but rather it came about as a genuine surprise, the unexpected consequence of the continuous focus on Spirit I've had to hold in my daily work and in my classes for many years. The more my work required me to shift my attention away from my own soul and ego dramas, and place my focus directly onto Spirit in service of others, the more blessings I personally received and the more expanded and transformed by the Holy Spirit I became.

Today, as a result of my routinely being connected with Spirit and open to blessings for so many years, my frequency has gradually elevated and I have transformed. I feel intimately connected with my Spirit, and I am continually flooded with daily blessings. Mine is not an intellectual state of mind. I *feel* God's holy force coursing through my entire being. And it isn't subtle. It is powerful.

I am humbled by the degree of blessings, healing, and insights made available to me through the Holy Spirit every day of my life, and at times I still find my ego and soul wondering how this can be so. The veil between my human and Divine Self has thinned substantially through my work with Spirit, and my ability to live in a higher and more loving vibration comes naturally. Words cannot fully describe this profound transformational occurrence, and yet it is so. I call this shift heaven on earth, because that is what it feels like.

It is not as though I do not face challenges on a soul level anymore. I do. I actually welcome these challenges now, and with the help of my blessings and Spirit, I find I am able to move through them quickly. This transformational shift from a soul-centered to a Spirit-centered life is now something that I am deeply committed to facilitating for everyone who is interested. In fact, I believe that it is my Spirit's greatest mission to do so. In reviewing my own joyful transformation, I am certain that this shift from personal, human self to Divine Spirit can come about for anyone. And I feel intuitively that we all must make this transformation sooner or later—no exceptions. Only now, the emphasis is on *sooner.*

I also consciously *know* that the transformation from soul to Spirit only comes about through practicing a daily, unwavering routine that focuses on Spirit and its blessings—nothing less, or more. And this is where I can help.

While I was blessed with guidance and support in my youth that opened the door from soul to Spirit for me, for which I am eternally grateful, I can honestly say that it has been only through my consistent effort and daily routine of placing my focus on Spirit over soul all these years, as well as receiving my blessings with an open heart, that real embodiment and trust in Spirit has occurred for me. The great gift of my life is that this un-wavering focus on Spirit has been *required* of me through my daily work with others. Had I not had this require-ment in place, I sincerely doubt the deep connection with Spirit and all its blessings that I now experience would have occurred.

If there is one thing that I aspire to achieve in my life, more than any other, it is to inspire in others the simplest, most compelling argument possible for establishing the same positive and self-loving routine of making daily contact with Source that was required of me over the years. Anyone who makes it a personal requirement to connect with their Spirit daily and open up to God's grace, guidance, and gifts will experience the same great healing and peace that I've experienced.

During the course of my life, I have studied with the best, most enlightened teachers. I have been mentored and guided by the most gifted of healers. I have traveled the world over and listened to the most dynamic and charismatic messengers. I have read thousands of books. I have sat in prayer and meditation. I have done all of this and more in pursuit of merging my soul with that of Source. And I have loved it all and will continue to seek and learn. It is my passion. It is my love. And yet, all of these paths lead back to the same unwavering truth.

It is only through one's consistent daily practice of connecting directly with Spirit and Source over soul that an incredible vibrational transformation is made possible. There is no shortcut or bypass.

The good news is that it is not difficult to connect to your Spirit (which is the Holy Spirit in you) and receive your blessings. You do not have to be a spiritual scholar or spend countless hours a day in meditation (although that is lovely and gives its own gifts if that speaks to you). You do not have to withdraw from the ordinary world or neglect your mundane responsibilities. You just have to embrace your Spirit and ask for God's blessings upon you *every single day.* Then be open and willing to receive your blessings, and no longer struggle to figure life out. That's it. It just takes both decision and consistency, and a few minutes every single day, until this focus becomes the very foundation of your life.

I guarantee that anyone who chooses to establish a consistent, devoted focus on Spirit over soul, on Source over ego-self, on blessings over struggle will eventually experience the same healing shift that I did. You will never again ask, "What is my soul's purpose?" You will be living it, which is to surrender soul to Spirit completely.

What Happens along the Way

Having worked with so many beautiful souls over the course of my life, leading them to the gifts and blessings of Spirit, I am aware that the ego and soul may have a few questions before they agree to cooperate. Namely, what can I expect if I make a commitment to surrender to Spirit? And, what will happen to me? So I will take a moment here to explain what your soul can expect.

First, your vibrational transformation from soul to Spirit will occur subtly, over time, as your routine begins to change your brain and reset your energetic frequency to a higher level. From your bones to your nervous system, to your mental and emotional self, to the very auric field surrounding you, all will slowly begin to resonate and sustain at a higher, more light-filled, fluid frequency. This shift is gradual so that your physical and energetic bodies can acclimate to this higher vibration and hold on to it in the denser, more constricted world in which we live.

With each day's repeated effort, you strengthen and reinforce your Spirit to subtly begin to dissolve the denser patterns of ego and soul that have a hold on you, both your own and those of others. Day by day you gradually deflect and eventually become unmoved to the pull of lower, victim oriented, negative forces all around.

The consequence of daily connection to Spirit is felt in gentle, subtle waves with an occasional *aha!* dotting the path, as opposed to a transformational lightning-bolt strike. You find yourself becoming more conscious of your choices and their creative power, good or bad. You naturally start to have an aversion to engaging in battles; your quick, knee-jerk negative reactions to life subside; and you begin to respond to life in a fresher, more-enlightened, nonreactive way. You cease to be so defensive and become more open to recognizing how your interactions with others serve as a reflection of your choices, perceptions, and behaviors, from which you can learn. You attract and create less drama, and draw more loving, positive experiences and people to your life. You become less hopeless and more optimistic, inspired, creative, and solution oriented in all areas of your life. Fear subsides as the dominant force controlling you, and true compassionate love for self and all takes its place. Day by day, with consistent attention to Spirit over soul, your true self emerges and you begin to live more authentically. You breathe in more deeply and relax. This transformational shift brings fundamental peace and contentment to you no matter what is happening around you.

The Three Blessings of Spirit

As I've mentioned earlier, you cannot effectively make this shift without God's help. Fortunately, the loving Universe bestows upon you great help in the form of three holy and powerful blessings to assist you on your journey home. These three blessings are *grace, guidance,* and *gifts.* These blessings act as your inner compass, your guiding light, and your inner resources as your soul finds its way back to Source.

Grace

The first blessing is *grace.* Grace is the God-given gift of divine support to help us rise above our human frailties and limitations. It is the equivalent of receiving from our great Creator a booster shot of "can-do" energy that mercifully frees us from our own self-created limitations and delivers us from the dramas and miseries we've created or face, and returns us to the path of healing and spiritual progress. Grace is the holy force that pulls us out of internal and external chaos; breaks us out of soul stagnation; illuminates our blind spots; gives us the power and strength to overcome pain, struggle, and dark nights of the soul; and keeps us moving toward our true nature as Spirit walking in God's holy light. The Holy Spirit bestows grace upon us all the time, but especially when we ask for it directly through prayer. As we increase our need for and awareness of God's grace in our lives, and dedicate ourselves to spreading God's grace wherever we go, the grace we receive is increased exponentially. With grace abounding in our lives, it becomes ever easier to connect with our Spirit, calm and advance our soul, quiet the ego, and flow in life as a Divine Being and child of light, as opposed to living as a confused and lost soul who struggles in the world.

Guidance

The second blessing that our all-loving Creator bestows upon us is *guidance*. We each have an internal energetic compass, known as *intuition* (meaning "inner teacher"), that is there to guide us moment by moment, day by day, to stay the course of our highest good and steer us toward full authenticity, wholeness, and inner peace. Intuition is the subtle, ever-present vibrational force that leads us toward that which most supports our soul's growth and away from that which will hinder it. Guidance leads us to greater creativity and capacity to love, and away from fear and destruction. Connecting with our inner guidance is *essential* to successfully connecting with our Spirit and living in our full authentic power as holy, empowered, co-creative beings.

Gifts

The third blessing bestowed upon us from the Holy Mother-Father God, Source of all life, is that of *gifts*. Gifts show up in our lives in four ways. The first way is that our loving Creator bestows certain gifts upon us. These are the strengths, talents, and virtues that we are personally endowed with when we are born and that we can develop in order to contribute to life as we grow. Using our gifts helps the world become a better, more loved, more beautiful, peaceful place, and that ultimately is our soul's purpose. The gifts we possess are said to be 1,000 in number, according to some Hindu traditions. I'm not certain whether this is true, but I do know that once we start to look for our gifts, we begin to recognize that we possess and experience far more gifts than we are generally aware of. We simply have to search a little deeper to find some of them.

Other people also shower gifts upon us. These gifts come in the way of assistance, contribution, support, and even, at times, aggravation and upset. No matter how these gifts show up when delivered by others, we can measurably see how they have undeniably furthered our life.

The third way that gifts show up in our lives is directly from the Creator. These gifts are provided in the form of synchronicities, wonderful surprises, unexpected positive turns of events, and what the unconscious among us call "luck." Finally, gifts also show up in our lives through our giving to others. When we extend ourselves by sharing our hearts and helping those around us, especially when we have no motive other than to be supportive, we receive gifts and blessings from those acts.

God sends us so many gifts every day that it is overwhelming, and as with noticing stars in the sky, once you begin to notice all the gifts in your life, the more you will see right before your eyes. And with gifts from God, just like discovering the stars in the sky, the more you notice their presence, the more you will realize that they were there all along. It was you who didn't notice.

All the ways in which blessings are showered upon us make life rich, meaningful, purposeful, and exciting. In fact, in receiving our three blessings—grace, guidance, and gifts—our lives become absolutely charmed. With such powerful protection, guidance, and support, every day welcomes us with a wide-open invitation to live and create at the highest, most-liberated level of being. Life becomes lighter as the light of our Spirit grows, and the heaviness of soul and ego begins to dissipate.

Our Blessings Are Abundant

The wonderful thing about our three blessings is that they are abundantly available to us as God's beloved children. It is only up to us to ask for, recognize, and accept them as the loving support they are. We do not need to struggle to earn our blessings, or "deserve" them. We must simply ask for them and say, "Yes, thank you," when they appear. The interesting thing is that our blessings usually show up when we least expect them. They often take us by surprise, catch us off guard, usually at the point when we feel as though we are at the end of our wits, trapped by circumstance, stuck in a corner, and demoralized, and cannot see our way ahead.

Accepting our blessings doesn't have to happen in dramatic moments, however. In fact, our blessings are intended to spare us from experiencing unnecessary dramas in life. They are given to keep us empowered and in co-creative flow instead. By becoming aware of your abundance of blessings from God, you increase the endless presence of Spirit in your life, and are benefited beyond your wildest dreams. It is simply up to you to recognize your need for these blessings, feel their presence all around, and accept their offerings.

Without grace and without using our guidance and gifts, our soul journey of struggle and drama will painfully drag on, and we will continue to feel our disconnection from Source. It is only by recognizing our blessings and relying on them to direct our lives that we can finally rise above the endless human struggle of the soul, ego, and the darkness of the world, and begin to live in the light and power of the Divine Spirit within each of us.

Now more than ever, it is time to access our blessings to the fullest in order to return to Source and free ourselves from the vicious and endless cycles of soul suffering that we have been struggling with forever. We are to stop trying to live as though we were separate and disconnected from our most Holy Mother-Father God and Creator Source, and begin to live in deep connection with the light and flow of our Spirit. This is exactly what these transformational times are all about, transforming from human, ego-based beings to divine, light-filled, Spirit-centered beings. Without God's blessings to help us, this is not possible. The time for struggle and suffering due to estrangement from our Source of life is over. But this is only possible if we choose to be free of the limitations of our ego-centered perceptions, patterns, and relentless soul dramas, and accept and embrace our God-given blessings that lead us home to Source.

How This Book and Meditation Program Will Help

This book and accompanying audio download are designed to help you establish a consistent daily routine of connecting to Source and calling in your Divine blessings of grace, guidance, and gifts to guide your human journey. The book is set up as a daily prayer book, a means of routine contact with Source that will keep you open to receiving your endless blessings, one day at a time. By following a simple daily routine as laid out in these pages, you will soon *feel* that you are indeed succeeding in connecting to Source and Spirit. You further reinforce this frequency by listening to the channeled 20-minute meditations whenever possible, but ideally right before going to sleep. (Instructions on how to download the meditation program are included at the end of this book.) In doing this every day, you will soon feel lighter and happier of heart, and have easier, stress-free days; and miracles upon miracles will appear in your life.

Establishing Your Routine

Each day, open the book to any page and read the "Message from Spirit" at the top. Next, speak out loud the morning prayer, affirmation, or invocation, as well as "Today's Mantra." Finally, silently read the blessing, several times if possible, until you *feel* its vibration pouring into your heart and filling you with light. When reading the blessing for the day, there is a place to fill in your name. The blessing becomes very personal and even more powerful when you actually write your name in the space provided in this section. The blessings have been channeled through me from Source to you, and seeing your name in writing leaves an even greater impact on your heart than just saying your name aloud does. This small act makes the blessing even more personal, and you feel the energy of the Creator touching your heart.

Be patient if you do not feel this blessed vibration pouring in right away. It is still happening. Your ego and soul vibration is initially so dense that it may block your feeling centers. Do not worry about this. This will change in time. Your efforts are still making a difference.

Once you read your message; speak your affirmation, prayer, or invocation; and receive your blessing, set about your day. Continue to empower your Spirit by repeating the simple mantra for the day, all day long. This will assure that you remain open to all your blessings throughout the day. Start the next day with a new message, and repeat the ritual. The entire process takes about five to ten minutes at the most. At the end of the day, just before bed if possible, listen to one of the meditations on the accompanying audio download. You can even fall asleep listening to the meditation if you want. It will still be heard by your subconscious mind, and speak to your soul and ego, reprogramming it to surrender to the Holy Spirit. Just relax and allow the meditation to work its magic. That's it.

By doing this each day, you create the foundation for a blessed day, guided by intuition, affirmed in the truth of your authentic Self, graced by the love and assistance of the Holy Spirit, and showered with gifts along your path. With this start, you will move through the day with a newfound yet solid sense of strength, confidence, and clarity, a sense of purpose and protection where there was once doubt, fear, and confusion.

Keep the book at your bedside, on your desk or coffee table, next to the bath, or anyplace where you will see it and reach for it every day. You may even want to carry it with you and refer to it throughout the day. If possible, recruit someone in your life to share the lesson; affirmation, prayer, or invocation; and blessing of the day with you. Have each person read the "Message from Spirit" respectively, and then say the affirmation, prayer, or invocation together. Finally have one person read the blessing to the other, and then vice versa.

If you are having an especially difficult day and are immersed in the thick of soul drama, read two or three "Messages from Spirit" at a time, or better yet, read one new lesson several times throughout the day. No matter how many "Messages" you read in a day or how many times you reread the same "Message" in a day, always start by first reading the lesson; then saying the affirmation, prayer, or invocation out loud; and finally silently reading the blessing. Be sure to reaffirm the day's mantra throughout the day. In following this practice, you will gradually elevate your vibration from that of soul to that of Spirit. Day by day your Spirit will become stronger and surround you with power. Each day begun this way will instantly become lighter and filled with more and more abundance and peace.

If you want to, you can start at the beginning of the book and work through it until the end. Or you can open up the book randomly each day and read the message that appears. If you open to the same "Message from Spirit" more than once or repeatedly, which often happens, you can be sure that this is no accident. Your Spirit really wants you to get that message. So read it slowly and take it in. Breathe deeply as you read and feel the message in your heart. Affirm the message with your own voice. Repeat the message with your daily mantra, knowing that the message is timely and important to receive.

Use this book daily for years to come. It is not the kind of book you read and put on the shelf. This is an interactive book that keeps strengthening your Spirit now and forever. Like a prayer book, it grows in meaning and power for you over time. Use it. Highlight what holds special meaning for you. Treasure it, and let it become your own bridge to heaven.

GRACE

Message from Spirit

It is Divine Grace that gives us the power to step past our comfort zone and live with both feet in. It is the grace of God that helps us face our controlling fears and give up our resistance to accepting all invitations, to letting go and enjoying our life experience fully. It is Divine Grace that escorts our defended pride away from our heart and leads it into the light of trust. Pray for the grace of God to free you from the prison of your own making.

Morning Prayer

Dear and Blessed Holy Mother-Father God,

I pray for your holy grace to help me get out of my own way and overcome any ignorance, fear, and resistance to life that I may consciously or unconsciously hold this day. I humbly ask for your holy grace to assist me in saying a wholehearted *yes!* to life as it unfolds before me. I pray for the grace to put two feet into every positive invitation, every opening, every opportunity I receive with 100 percent willingness to fully commit to, experience, and enjoy my life as a protected, illuminated Divine Being. I pray for your holy grace to enable me to drop my unconscious, ego-based defenses, prideful posturing, and limiting ideas and beliefs, and to help me fully open my heart to receive more of your love, more of your light, more enthusiasm, and more confidence as I move through this day.

I ask for your grace to help me surrender all illusion of control that I may try to exert on others this day and instead turn my awareness inward and open my heart to follow your subtle promptings as they appear before me, step by step. I humbly ask to be a channel of your holy grace with all people I encounter today. I pray for your holy grace to flow uninterrupted through my words, actions, thoughts, and feelings, helping me to open the hearts of those with whom I interact though your bright, loving light flowing through every cell of my entire being. Please, Holy Mother-Father God, bestow your holy grace upon me this day so that I may be an agent of your never-ending love and peace on this beautiful and blessed planet.

I fully open my heart to receive your holy grace this day. In humble gratitude and confidence, I thank you in advance for answering my prayer.

Today's Mantra

Holy Mother-Father God, I humbly ask for your grace to help me be fully open to all blessings of this day.

Your Personal Blessing

Today, _____ (your name), I, your ever-loving Holy Mother-Father God, Creator of the Universe, and Source of all life, bless your Spirit with my benevolent, unceasing grace, thus giving you the ability to spontaneously, freely, and fully open your heart and confidently step into the day's experiences with full commitment, glorious enthusiasm, and willing participation to receive all of the gifts this day brings to you.

I bless your Spirit with my omnipresent grace to empower you with the ability to fully surrender your ego's control and prideful resistance to all unfamiliar invitations and to move beyond your comfort zone and learn from this day's experiences something new and life-affirming for your Spirit. I bless and fill your Spirit with my grace in your every thought, word, deed, and feeling so that you remain ever mindful and accepting of your power as a Divine Being and a true co-creator with me in the Universe.

I bless you and fill your Spirit with my holy grace to take maximum joy in this day's unfolding, meeting every challenge it presents with heartfelt willingness to see and embrace the light, lessons, love, and growth it offers. I bless and fill your Spirit with my grace to speak with love, act with love, and be filled with love as you interact with my other divine children on your path. I bless and fill your Spirit with my holy grace to be free, step out of your mental prison of limited ideas, erroneous beliefs, and false ego-perceptions, and be filled instead with the sudden enlightenment and profound understanding of a deeper, more profound holy wisdom that lies within you as my holy child. By my decree as your Holy Mother-Father God, in answer to your prayer I bless and fill your Spirit with my grace to accomplish your very best this day and to do so with joy and peace of mind.

And so it is in my name, the Holy Mother-Father God who created you and loves you unconditionally; the light, love, and healing of Christ; and the power of the Holy Spirit that lives and moves in your being.

◄ ✿ ►

Message from Spirit

Grace takes us to a place of deeper honesty with ourselves and others, and frees us from the lies our ego tells us, lies that keep us from living the full, authentic expression of pure, divine nature. Grace turns the light on in the darkened mind and shows us that there is really nothing to be afraid of after all. Ask for God's grace to help you step toward your heart instead of run away from it. Grace is a personal visitation in your life from God. It is a sudden and liberating force that frees us from the fear, attachment, control, and entitlement that possess us at any given moment. Grace breaks us out of the jail of the ego and restores us to the throne of Universal awareness and true higher power.

Morning Prayer

Dear Holy Mother-Father God,

I humbly ask you to bestow your all-empowering grace upon me this day so that I will become more honest with others and, most of all, with myself. I ask for your grace to help me stop placing blame on others or myself for things that have been difficult or painful in my life, and begin to gracefully experience life free from the attacks, lies, shame, guilt, and anger my ego casts upon my life events. I ask for your loving grace to enlighten my dark and angry thoughts, and free me from the illusion of victimhood that separates me from you, my all-loving Creator and Source.

I pray for your holy and benevolent blessing of grace to give me the courage to step in the direction of my heart's desire without hesitation or fear. Help me not to succumb to the endless stream of excuses and reasons that my ego offers for avoiding my authentic path. I ask for your grace this day to help me stop talking about what I am going to do and, instead, actually do it. I ask for your loving and merciful grace to help me remain conscious and mindful of your loving presence in my life, blessing me over and over with your loving gifts. I ask for your most holy grace to help me to trust others and ask them for their help and support, rather than arrogantly try to act as if I have it all "under control." I ask for your holy grace to help me to live a life of integrity this day, thinking, feeling, acting, and speaking in alignment with my authentic Self, and not surrendering to the negative influences of others or that of my fearful ego that encourages me to act in opposition to my truth.

I ask for your holy grace to keep me mindful of my true place in the Universe as your holy and beloved child and servant, and to stay faithful to my inner and outer work as a Spiritual light worker, who is here to bring more love and peace to this beautiful and blessed planet this day. I thank you in advance for answering my prayer.

Today's Mantra

Dear Beloved God, please give me the grace to be authentic this day.

Your Personal Blessing

Today, _____ (your name), I, your ever-loving Holy Mother-Father God, Creator of the Universe, and Source of all life, bless and fill your Spirit with my benevolent, unceasingly loving grace, thus giving you the ability to be unwaveringly honest with yourself and others in every way.

I bless and fill your Spirit with my holy grace so that you can be faithful to your heart's desire, never doubting its value and merit to you and this planet, and doing all in your power to make your dreams become reality. I bless and fill your Spirit with my holy and benevolent grace to reclaim all lost pieces of your soul, restoring you on this day to full integrity and wholeness as I, your Creator and Source, designed you to be. I bless and fill your Spirit with my loving grace to stand in the whirlwind of those who would make you doubt yourself, and quietly and clearly state your truth without diminishing yourself or your words out of fear of judgment, rejection, or retribution.

I bless and fill your Spirit with my grace to educate your rational mind about my higher power and awareness working through you so that you can look past appearances and see the deeper meaning in all that unfolds before you this day. I bless and fill your Spirit with my ceaseless gift of grace to give you the power to walk upright and in peace, even when others reject you or your dreams. I bless and fill your Spirit with *my holy and unceasing, loving grace this day as I enlighten your thoughts with inspiration, vision, intuition, and insight, shedding light on your path each step of the way this day.*

I bless and fill your Spirit with grace to move through this day with a clear mind and a light heart, open to new ideas and intuitions, and quickly willing to follow the path that runs closest to your heart, even when that calls for a sudden change of direction.

I bless and fill your Spirit with the grace to be courageously truthful with those who are not yet awake, loving yet direct in stepping away from all conversation and behaviors that disparage or disrespect anyone or that fail to recognize holy light in all beings. I bless and fill your Spirit with the grace to be a grounded steward of my light and love, offering clear direction and support to those who need a hand, and loving reassurance to them to stay true to their dreams and the desires of their heart. I bless and fill your Spirit with my holy grace to confidently and fearlessly walk hand in hand with me, your loving Creator, as your closest companion and most loving support, this and every day.

And so it is in my name, the Holy Mother-Father God who created you and loves you unconditionally; the light, love, and healing of Christ; and the power of the Holy Spirit that lives and moves in your being.

Message from Spirit

Grace is the secret ingredient we need in order to live up to our highest potential and to fully realize our heart's desires. We are not designed to live apart from the Source of all life, the Holy Mother-Father God who bestows upon us the power, creativity, and skill we need in order to succeed in life. Humble your ego and ask for God's grace to lift you up and deliver you to a lighter, more authentic, more natural joy than your ego can ever deliver. Then be still and allow your heart to receive it.

Morning Prayer

Holy Mother-Father God, Blessed Creator and Source of all life,

I humbly ask for your grace this day to be the best possible self I can be in all of my doings, in all that I speak, all that I think, and all that I feel. I ask for your benevolent grace to help me express my creativity and jump-start my energy to move in the direction of my highest good, leaving in my wake beautiful creations that are reflective of my authentic Spirit, benevolent to this planet and filled with your most holy light and love.

I humbly ask you to grant my Spirit the grace to be filled with a light heart this day, casting aside all shadows and dreariness that are directed toward my Spirit from the negative and unconscious world around me, and to recognize and celebrate instead all the wonderful gifts and blessings laid at my feet and on my path every moment of every day, making my life easier and more magical and charmed than ever before. Grace my Spirit with the humility to cease foolishly trying to exercise control over life and especially those around me, and to quietly allow my day to unfold in harmony and with respect for your own graceful divine plan, without interference, disruption, or disturbance from my ego.

Please grace my Spirit with the resourcefulness and creativity to respond to all challenges upon my path this day with positive and welcoming energy, allowing me to exercise lucid reasoning and make insightful decisions inspired by you, my most holy Creator, so that I may quickly turn around all difficult situations to flow in the direction of positive solutions that bring the highest good for all those involved now and in the future.

Please grace my Spirit with laughter as I draw all my needs—body, mind, and soul—from your eternal well of Divine Source, knowing that there is no end to what I can access from your loving waters of life and that therefore I have nothing to fear. Grace my Spirit with love for my work this day, and awaken in my Spirit the necessary skills I must demonstrate so that I am able to do masterful work in your honor and in your name.

I thank you in advance and with all my heart for hearing and answering my prayer, and I joyfully await your grace this day.

Today's Mantra

Blessed Creator, grant my Spirit the grace to peacefully accept everything that comes my way and to do and be my best with it.

Your Personal Blessing

Today, _____ (your name), I, your ever-loving Holy Mother-Father God, Creator of the Universe, and Source of all life, bless and fill your Spirit with my benevolent, unceasingly loving grace to experience a day filled with a quiet, calm, peaceful heart and a lighthearted joy.

I bless and fill your Spirit with my grace to breathe and relax into the moments unfolding before you, watchful and discerning, and detached from the emotional waves coming toward you from others. I bless and fill your Spirit with my grace so that you feel deeply supported by me, your Divine Source, the Holy Mother-Father God and your loving Creator. I bless and fill your Spirit with the grace to remain centered and clear, focused on your work with devotion and care, doing your best in service to humanity and with love for all whom you serve this day.

I bless and fill your Spirit with my grace to protect you from any and all negative energies and emotional drama flowing from unconscious people toward you or around you, making you immune to all that could potentially demoralize you, make you doubt yourself, or disturb your peace in any way. I bless and fill your Spirit with my grace so that you will be filled with song and music as you move through this day, bringing cheer to your heart and sweetness to your voice. I bless and grace your Spirit to see the value to your soul's growth in all things that unfold before you this day. I bless and fill your Spirit with my grace to take no offense to anything or anyone so that you may flow through this day in uninterrupted peace of mind, calm and grounded in your body. I bless and fill your Spirit with the grace to be inspired as you work, and to do so at the highest level of skill and mastery so that your efforts reflect your best talents and intentions. I bless and fill your Spirit with my grace to take command of your thoughts, emotions, and expression so that you think, feel, and move in a state of fluid ease, expressing your most authentic Self and bringing forward from others their most authentic selves as well, thus opening the way for loving interactions, filled with laughter and creative satisfaction for all. I bless and fill your Spirit with the grace to set side any impulsive, ego-centered reactions to others who might irritate you this day, and to be forgiving, tolerant, patient, and humorous with those around you, willing to overlook the mistakes of others, as well as those you make yourself. I bless and grace your Spirit to move through this day enthusiastically and with great appreciation of all my gifts to you.

And so it is in my name, the Holy Mother-Father God who created you and loves you unconditionally; the love, light, and healing of Christ; and the Power of the Holy Spirit that lives and moves in your being.

Message from Spirit

Grace surrounds us all the time. It is seen in the rising sun. It is felt from the warmth of its rays. It is heard in the song of the bird, the crash of an ocean wave, the whistle of the wind through the rustling trees. Grace can be found in the scent of a flower and the taste of fresh fruit. It can be felt in the touch of a loved one or the softness of a feather. Grace is everywhere. One only needs the heart to allow it in. Grace is there for you. Do not let your ego hide from it. Be grateful and let it in.

Morning Prayer

Holy Mother-Father God, blessed Creator, and Source of all life,

I humbly ask for your grace this day to open my heart and mind to the abundance of love and sweetness that you make available to me in all ways. I ask for your benevolent grace to help me to fully witness your presence all around me this day—in this sunshine on my face, the song of the birds in the trees, the beautiful smell of fresh flowers wafting through the air as I pass by your lovely gardens, the flow of fresh water over my skin as I bathe in preparation for the day. I humbly ask for you to grant my Spirit the grace to be filled with deep gratitude for the beautiful planet that I walk on, the trees, flowers, plants, birds, and animals that bring so much beauty, joy, and comfort.

Grace my Spirit with the awareness to slow down in my actions this day and savor the blessings bestowed upon me. Grace me with the presence of mind to chew slowly, and fully taste all the lovely and nutritious food you lovingly set before me on this day. Grant me the ability to eat with grace, not too fast and not too much, thus nourishing my body without overtaxing it with excess. Please grace my Spirit with clear discernment to choose that which supports and strengthens it, in the foods I choose to eat, the things I choose to drink, the conversations I choose to engage in, the materials I choose to read, the entertainment I choose to watch, so that all that I put into my body, mind, and soul supports my Spirit at the highest level and keeps me healthy, strong, peaceful, and lighthearted.

I humbly ask that you grace my Spirit with a deep sense of gratitude for all that I am given, and keep my thoughts free from fear concerning all that I may not have or be given. Grace my Spirit with love for life this day, and awaken in my Spirit a sense of fulfillment and abundance so that I may never again worry for my needs to be filled.

I thank you in advance and with all my heart for hearing and answering my prayer, and I joyfully await your grace this day.

Today's Mantra

Most loving Mother-Father God, please bestow upon me the grace to be aware of all the loving gifts you shower upon me this day.

Your Personal Blessing

Today, _____ (your name), I, your ever-loving Holy Mother-Father God, Creator of the Universe, and Source of all life, bless and fill your Spirit with my benevolent, unceasingly loving grace to become fully aware of my loving presence surrounding you this day.

I bless and fill your Spirit with my grace to breathe in the sweet smell of flowers in the air, refreshing you with their cleansing and uplifting essence. I bless and fill your Spirit with my grace to feel my presence in the sunlight dancing on your face, the sweet sound of the birds singing to you from the treetops, and my healing love sent in the soft breeze dancing across your cheeks. I bless and fill your Spirit with the grace to be mindful of the great blessing of food and drink placed before you this day, and I share my grace so that you may enjoy all the bounty before you without the need to overindulge or choose unwisely in the ways in which you nourish your body.

I bless and grace your Spirit with the power to transform all that you eat and drink into fuel for your most energized state of being, while eliminating the rest so that your physical body is balanced, light, and free of excess, and so that it feels healthy, strong, and beautiful, as I made it and intended it to serve you. I bless and fill your Spirit with my grace so that you can be free of all anxiety for any need that you may have, *and allow your emotions and thoughts to rest in the assurance that I am here to provide as your authentic needs arise.*

I bless and fill your Spirit with my grace so that you will be uplifted by the beauty of nature, and I instill in you the desire to shine upon the world the beauty I have placed in your heart. I bless and fill your Spirit with the grace to humble and quiet your controlling ego, so that my divine presence may be the guiding force in your life. I bless and fill your Spirit with my grace to easily and quickly refuse to partake in any activity, however benign or harmless it may appear, that does not respect and honor the grace and holiness in you and in all people. This includes engaging in callous, mean-spirited conversations, gossiping, fear mongering, or casting about negative and demoralizing words or prognostications.

I bless and fill your Spirit with the grace to fearlessly trust in the goodness of this world and the people in it, and to speak up and share positive feedback and support with all those with whom you are blessed to interact this day. I bless and fill your Spirit with my grace to take charge of your ego and train it to turn to me for guidance, rather than fight others and run away from my light and love. I bless and fill your Spirit with the grace to take time this day to relax and enjoy the beauty all around you. I bless and grace your Spirit to be fully available this day to all the beauty and love coming to you from this planet and the people surrounding you.

And so it is in my name, the Holy Mother-Father God who created you and loves you unconditionally; the love, light, and healing of Christ; and the power of the Holy Spirit that lives and moves in your being.

Message from Spirit

Grace is food from heaven to feed and grow the Holy Spirit within you. It is grace that gives you the power to forgive when you are still freshly and deeply wounded, and the ability to refrain from judgment or counter-attack when you've been hurt. Grace gives you the ability to not take personally the most personal of assaults on your being, mind, and body, and to still see, accept, and love the Spirit within the attacker. Grace is the only force that allows one to live as the Divine Beings we are naturally designed to be, as opposed to ego-based, fearful, angry, hurt, and separated-from-Source human beings. Grace is the only way to freedom. God's grace is the only way to peace.

Morning Prayer

Dear Holy Mother-Father God,

I humbly ask you to bestow your all-empowering grace upon me this day so that I find the power to forgive those who have hurt or injured me in the past, even though I still feel the pain of their injuries to me. Allow me the grace to stop dwelling on the past, and to release all moments from my mind and emotions where I have perceived myself to be wronged and felt hurt, whether or not the events that passed were meant to personally assault me. I humbly ask for your holy grace to give me the ability to let bygones be bygones, and to free my mind permanently of any memory of wrongdoing, whether at my expense or caused by me.

I ask for your holy grace to release me from all guilt or shame that is the result of my own wrongdoing or wrong thinking in the past so that I may forgive myself fully and learn from my mistakes but not be held hostage by them. I ask for your loving grace to release from my heart all resentments that may lurk there toward others so that I know that though mistakes were made, they were made by those who are, like me, students of life, learning to live in light as opposed to being controlled by the darkness and confusion of the frightened ego. I pray for your holy and benevolent blessing of grace to give me the peace of mind that comes from forgiving the past and from bearing no grudges toward those who I feel may have caused me intentional pain, knowing that we make these errors when we are disconnected from you, our loving Source of life.

I ask for your grace this day to help me ask for the forgiveness of others toward whom I have behaved poorly or in an unloving, unfair, or unkind manner, finding the courage to admit my mistakes and make amends where appropriate without hiding from my actions or denying my behavior. I ask for your loving and merciful grace to help me find the gift behind all negative or painful experiences from the past, so I may understand that all things occur in life in the interest of growing my soul and that, in fact, there are no true mistakes, only lessons that I must learn. I ask for your most holy grace to help me live in the moment and let the past go once and for all so that I may spend my day fully available to the gifts of the moment. Free me, through your gift of grace, from all thoughts of revenge or victimhood that I may hold on to, and help me see the light and blessing in all events that have in the past caused pain, either on my part or to me.

I ask for your holy grace so that I may live and let live, refraining from any judgment toward others' behavior or the belief that I may know better than they do how to live their lives. Most of all, I ask for your holy grace to forgive me of all my past mistakes and errors, in this and all my past lives, including all agreements, contracts, vows, and commitments I have made that have not been centered in my heart and most authentic Self.

I thank you in advance for my blessing of your Divine Grace, knowing that without your grace, forgiveness is not fully possible.

Today's Mantra

Dear Beloved God, please give me the grace to forgive everyone, everything, every time.

Your Personal Blessing

Today, _____ (your name), I, your ever-loving, Holy Mother-Father God, Creator of the Universe, and Source of all life, bless and fill your Spirit with my benevolent, loving grace and fill you with a forgiving Spirit in all matters in your life.

I bless and fill your Spirit with my grace to release you from all past injuries and to take no offense, bear no grudges, and hold no resentments toward those who have caused you pain. I *bless and fill your Spirit, _____ (your name), with my grace to let the past go and to live fully and freely in the moment. I bless your Spirit with the grace to view all of your life events from the perspective of your Higher Self, learning from your experiences and being free of their negative impact on your emotions, thoughts, and body. I bless your Spirit to be filled with my grace to fully and freely forgive you of all past mistakes, and to find the courage and strength of character to correct what you can with sincere apology and amendments, giving the rest to me to cleanse and erase.*

I bless your Spirit with my grace to free your memory from all past hurt and psychic injury so that your heart may be fully open and receptive to all the goodness that life brings you this day. I bless and fill your Spirit with my grace to forgive all past self-injury, and the power and love to respect your Spirit fully and lovingly in this moment. I bless and fill your Spirit with my grace so that you see past all poor behaviors and recognize the light of the Holy Spirit inside each person you encounter, even those who have lost touch with their light and behave from the darkness of their fears.

I bless and fill your Spirit with my grace to find peace in your heart where injury and upset once took place, and to be unable to remember injury so as to protect your inner peace and keep your holy calm intact and undisturbed. I bless and fill your Spirit with my grace to take no offense or react negatively to the behaviors of others, even when they are unjust or offensive. I bless and fill your Spirit with the grace to speak with kindness and calm, centered clarity, and to establish and hold unwavering self-respecting boundaries so as to not invite offensive behavior or personal violation upon you on the part of others. I bless and grace your Spirit to move through this day with serenity and peace.

And so it is in my name, the Holy Mother-Father God who created you and loves you unconditionally; the love, light, and healing of the Christ; and the power of the Holy Spirit that lives and moves in your being.

Message from Spirit

Grace gives us patience, both with ourselves and with others. Grace assists us in honestly assessing our weaknesses and lies, and leads us back to light rather than mercilessly condemning and shaming our inadequacies, banishing us into further darkness. Grace invites us to live in integrity and wholeness, fully in the moment, as opposed to living in fragmented pieces, looking for those we've lost, and feeling scattered about the past and stuck. Grace brings us into a state of healing and makes us the healer of others as well—not by words or deeds, but simply by our vibration of wholeness. Grace heals.

Morning Prayer

Dear Holy Mother-Father God,

I humbly ask you to bestow your all-empowering grace upon me this day so that I may live in full integrity with my Spirit.

Allow me the grace to pause before I speak so that I may communicate with clarity and purpose this day, expressing what I truly want to express, and not mindlessly casting about meaningless words that do not reflect my authentic Self. Please also grant my Spirit the grace to listen deeply to others as they speak to me, opening my heart and mind so that I may truly understand their intentions and needs, and to not filter their words with what I want hear to accommodate my ego's point of view, but rather to hear with genuine interest, willingness to respect and learn from another, and, above all, real love.

Please give me the grace to have compassion and love for myself this day, and to hold kind and accepting thoughts toward myself, especially when I feel insecure or make mistakes, so that I am able to be open, kind, and gentle with others because my heart is at peace and I feel safe in my own skin. I humbly ask for the grace to focus fully on the blessings of this day, and to refuse to entertain negative or condemning thoughts of the past that serve no useful or loving purpose and keep me stuck in shame and broken pieces, missing the value of the moment.

I ask for your holy grace to keep me centered and whole as I move through this day, free of all addictions, or unconscious and compulsive behaviors, finding my needs easily and comfortably met without anxiety or attachment to things or people who are not my true Source of support. I ask for the grace to be patient with myself and with others this day so that I do not unnecessarily put stress or strain on my nervous system when things do not go my way or as planned. I ask for the grace to laugh instead of get angry or worked up when I encounter difficult or stressful situations. Please grace me with the ability to be a healing force and a bright light of positive and loving energy around the people I encounter this day.

I am eternally grateful to you for hearing my prayer and for granting my Spirit the grace I need to live as a Divine Being in human form.

Today's Mantra

Grace me with patience and mindfulness to live peacefully this day.

Your Personal Blessing

Today, _____ (your name), I, *your ever-loving Holy Mother-Father God, Creator of the Universe, and Source of all life, bless and fill your Spirit with my benevolent, loving grace so that you remain grounded and faithful to your most authentic Self throughout this day.*

I bless and grace your Spirit with the ability to pause and breathe before you speak so that your words are mindful and resonant with your truth and your heart. I bless and grace your Spirit to slow down, and to breathe and reflect before you act so that your behavior reflects your most authentic Self and is not merely ego-based reactions that take you away from your truth.

I bless and grace your Spirit, _____ (your name), to bring love and light to all who are in your company, activating in them their own love and light, so that you are a true bringer of blessings wherever you go this day. I bless and grace your Spirit to speak kindly and lovingly to yourself this day, so you can move freely and without fear of being attacked by your ego or shamed by guilt for what are normal human mistakes. I bless and grace your Spirit with the ability to retrieve all lost fragments of your soul, bound in past hurtful experiences or psychic wounding, so that you may feel whole and complete now, in present time.

I bless and grace your Spirit with the honesty to admit your weaknesses and mistakes, and to ask for help so that you can do better without hesitation, insecurity, or false pride. I bless and grace your beautiful Spirit with positive focus, open-mindedness, and a willingness to learn to do things in a better or different way when you receive feedback that the way you are presently doing things is not working. I bless and grace your Spirit with freedom from the past so that all shadows and darkness are dispelled, and you are basked in my light and love this day. I bless and grace your Spirit to be aware of and respectful of your true boundaries and genuine needs so that you act in accordance with your highest good, and clearly reject, quickly and without drama, all that does not serve you.

I bless and grace your Spirit with loving companions, both on the earthly plane and in the heavenly realms, surrounding you with humor, friendship, guidance, laughter, ease, and flow throughout this day. I bless and grace your Spirit with confidence and peace in being your best and most loving self with every person you encounter, speaking your truth, sharing your real feelings, and asking for what you need in a calm and grounded way, knowing that all needs are known by me, your Source, Holy Mother-Father God, and will be answered.

And so it is in my name, the Holy Mother-Father God who created you and loves you unconditionally; the love, light, and healing of the Christ; and the power of the Holy Spirit that lives and moves in your being.

◄ ▨ ►

Message from Spirit

Grace gives us the ability to stop and rest after experiencing chaos. Grace brings us relief and the ability to surrender our loud cries of fear into the healing quiet of silence. Grace, God's personal support in our lives, guides us through the upheavals and chaos of life, and gives us the strength to accept rather than fight what is so. Grace allows us to believe that all that unfolds is for the ultimate good of the soul, even though it may be painful, disappointing, disruptive, and even, at times, deathly. Grace makes certain that all that is taken away is refilled with new life, new love. Grace is our refuge. Grace brings the new dawn.

Morning Prayer

Dear Holy Mother-Father God,
I pray that you bestow your all-empowering grace upon me this day and bring quiet to my anxious heart. I humbly ask for your grace so that I remain grounded and steady during these transitional times, and so that I keep from succumbing to the fears and chaos that my mind creates as I encounter unknown, unfamiliar, and unsteady situations. Please give me the grace to accept the way things are and to weather disappointment with dignity and trust, knowing in my heart and higher mind

that the way things turn out is in accordance with your divine plan. Please grant me the grace to surrender what is being removed or eliminated from my life with complete cooperation, and endow me with the confidence to know that for whatever life takes away, it brings back in renewal and unseen bounty, and I am safe even in the midst of great change and disruption.

I ask you, Holy Mother-Father God, to give me the grace I need to remain a steady and stable force for those I love when they, too, face disruption and upheaval, so that I may keep them calm and centered in the faith that all will be okay in the end. Surround my eyes with grace so that I may look away from what unnecessarily frightens me and takes away my strength. Surround my ears with your grace so that I may tune out all menacing broadcasts that reflect others' confusion and bear no witness to the truth that you are forever present and all is well. Give me the grace to be a welcome presence for those in pain so that I may ease their distress and bring relief to their troubled minds.

Let me walk through this day, facing all that unfolds, especially that which is challenging and unexpected, with grounded and confident faith that your holy plan is behind everything that occurs and that in every situation lies a hidden gift, waiting for me to discover it. I ask for your grace as I experience release and surrender to all that is dying in my life, knowing that there is no death of the Spirit and that even though forms change, we continue to grow and expand in our light bodies forever.

I thank you in advance for hearing my prayer and for your grace as I walk through transitional times. By your grace I know that I will meet the day and all its ups and downs with deep breaths and an open and receptive heart, listening for your guidance and trusting in your plan. I am grateful now and always.

Today's Mantra

Grant me the grace to accept life as it unfolds today.

Your Personal Blessing

Today, _____ (your name), I, your ever-loving Holy Mother-Father God, Creator of the Universe, and Source of all life, bless and fill your Spirit with my benevolent, loving grace so that you may face the changes and shifts that this day brings with quiet resolve and surrender to my holy plan.

I bless and grace your Spirit with flexibility and adaptability to move and flow with the changes of this day without resistance, rejection, or fear. I bless and grace your Spirit with dignity under fire, and give you the courage to face all loss with ease and a deep willingness to detach and let go, allowing for a greater experience to take the place of the one you are surrendering in the moment. I bless and grace your Spirit to be free of all need or desire to try to control events or people, or bend them to your personal will and against my divine plan. I bless and grace your Spirit to easily detach from your own ego-based agendas and to be open to new information and changes in plan with enthusiasm and cooperation.

I bless and grace your Spirit, _____ (your name), to be surrounded in my divine light throughout this day, activating the light and peace in others as they interact with you. I grace and bless your Spirit to fully feel all of your emotions, including those of grief, disappointment, sadness, frustration, indignation, and even anger, and then, just as quickly, through the aid of your breath, let these emotions leave your body, allowing you to regain your peace and serenity. I bless and grace your Spirit with the fortitude to withstand all losses or disappointments you are met with this day without collapsing into your emotions, knowing that whatever does not go your way does so for the benefit of your soul's growth, and that in due time, the greater plan will be revealed to you. I bless and grace your beautiful Spirit with the ability to accept rather than fight all that unfolds this day, using what is so to guide you to make the best, most grounded, well-informed decisions in response to what is happening.

I bless and grace your Divine and Holy Spirit to fearlessly look at all that is dying in this hour, on this day, knowing that in truth, all that dies is only changing forms and returning to pure energy and Spirit, only to be reborn again. I bless and grace your Spirit with the honesty to allow that which needs to be surrendered to die in your life without guilt, control, or resistance to its natural life cycle, to move on from your life as you know it, and to be reborn in accordance with my divine plan.

And so it is in my name, the Holy Mother-Father God who created you and loves you unconditionally; the love, light, and healing of the Christ; and the power of the Holy Spirit that lives and moves in your being.

Message from Spirit

Grace brings laughter where fear would have us re-coil in silence. Grace tickles our funny bone and keeps us from falling into the abyss of taking ourselves, or life, too seriously. Grace chases our devils of illusion away, and ushers in angels of clarity and light in their place. Grace reveals the truth of our infinite and holy nature, and shoos away the detractors of Spirit and the destroy-ers of life.

Morning Prayer

Dear Holy Mother-Father God,

I pray for you to bestow your all-empowering grace upon me this day so that I may look life in the eye and find the humor in all that unfolds before me. Please bring me the grace to see with my divine eyes into the deeper meaning behind all events occurring to me and around me, knowing that life is truly a divine theater and that all shall eventually pass.

Grace me with the ability to laugh at myself and at all my mistakes. Please let me take nothing that occurs today too seriously, and grace me with the wisdom to chuckle rather than react defensively at any affront to my perceptions or ego. Let me enjoy the silliness of life and appreciate the creative efforts of all the people I interact with this day.

Allow me the grace to go with the flow and surrender my ego's sensitivities over to a good-natured response to all that does not initially please me. Grace me with the ability to be an earth angel of goodwill and good humor this day, easing the tension and stress carried in the minds and bodies of those I meet.

Grant me the grace to smile at life, as opposed to struggle with it, and help me seize every opportunity to escape my own heavy dramas and turn them into comic relief. Let me walk in your grace this day and not sweat the small stuff, even when it doesn't feel so small. Grace my thoughts with delightful messages, and surround me with the best of your angelic clowns this day. I ask you, Holy Mother-Father God, to grace my day with entertaining experiences and the blessing of music, dance, art, and song.

Please give me the grace to release all resentments I may hold, and allow me to finally recognize beyond all doubt or confusion the futility and silliness of allowing my ego to rob me of a single moment of joy. Please grace me with a twinkle in my eye and a smile on my lips this day, so that I feel your holy goodness and love present in all things and people. Allow me to share and activate in others, through your loving grace, a spark for life in all the ways it unfolds this day. Let me make a game of this day so that I play with the angels, enjoy my fellow humans, bask in nature, and refresh my Spirit with your love.

I thank you for hearing my prayer this day and for the grace you rain upon my life, which allows me the adventure of discovering how to live as a Divine Being and co-creator with you, Holy Mother-Father God, on earth. I am grateful to you now and always.

Today's Mantra

Holy Mother-Father God, please grant me the grace to live lightly.

Your Personal Blessing

Today, _____ (your name), I, your ever-loving Holy Mother-Father God, Creator of the Universe, and Source of all life, bless and fill your Spirit with my benevolent, loving grace so that you may find yourself filled with lighthearted good nature and an easygoing, relaxed flow.

I bless and fill your Spirit with the grace to let things roll off your back, to excuse and overlook the irritations of others, and to attract all manner of joyful and entertaining diversions throughout your day. I grace and fill your Spirit with the deep insight to instantly cast off all fearful illusions, and to laugh out loud at what otherwise may try to frighten or discourage you. I bless and grace your Spirit with the ability to experience no insult at even the most offensive or insulting attacks launched your way so that you smile, forgive, and return dark energy with lightheartedness, thus turning around the intentions of those who may attempt to rob you of your energy and power, or make you doubt yourself in any way.

I bless and grace your Spirit, _____ (your name), with a brilliant, compelling, and attractive vibration that emanates from your every cell and draws those around you, even those who might otherwise try to condemn or harshly judge you, to help, support, and recommend you *in every way. Like the Pied Piper of Delight, I grace you with the power to draw others to your light and laughter, thus creating a wave of joy wherever you go this day. Like the sun rising after a turbulent storm, I grace your Spirit with the power to clear all negativity in the atmosphere wherever you stand, and to banish all stress and tension in the air wherever you move.*

I bless and grace you with the best of my muses from heaven, filling your mind with the most creative, original, clever ideas; new perspectives; and silly notions that make your day endlessly entertaining. I grace and bless your Spirit with the power to stop negative conversation and grumblings with your quick wit and comic antics so that you help others break free of their negative patterns, habits, and behaviors that keep them from living their authentic Spirit. I bless and grace your Divine and Holy Spirit with pure happiness at being alive this day so that you waste not a single moment on a distracting dark thought or fear.

I grace your Spirit with the ability to spread the light and love wherever you walk and with all whom you meet, so their day is brightened for having been in your company. I bless and grace your Spirit with amnesia for past grudges and wounding memories so that those experiences are instead reframed with objectivity, humor, and detachment. I grace your Spirit with the angels of laughter, who will tickle your funny bone and amuse you all day.

And so it is in my name, the Holy Mother-Father God who created you and loves you unconditionally; the love, light, and healing of the Christ; and the power of the Holy Spirit that lives and moves in your being.

Message from Spirit

Grace brings us together when we want to run and hide. Grace fills our emptiness when we feel alone and unworthy. Grace sweetens our journey with gifts and blessings when we least expect support. Grace brings friendship and love and family when we feel isolated and overwhelmed. Grace makes us aware of all the riches given to us. With God's grace, life becomes a joyous journey. Without it, it is an unbearable and meaningless burden. Grace is an unexpected source and force of love that allows us to become more conscious, secure, creative, and loving.

Morning Prayer

Dear Holy Mother-Father God,

I pray for you to bestow your all-empowering grace upon me this day to keep my heart open and my Spirit in charge even in the face of sudden or unexpected loss.

Grace me with the faith to remember my own goodness in those moments when I am tempted to judge myself harshly or condemn myself to live without forgiveness as not being worthy of love. I ask for your grace to keep my Spirit from collapsing into my own dark emotions when life becomes difficult, to help me to remain centered and calm, and trust in your love and light to get me through the dark moments. Grace my Spirit with the ability to feel deep and infinite gratitude for your ceaseless blessings upon me this day, and especially for those blessings that come in the form of loving friendships and comforting companionship.

Grace my heart with abundant love and affection for life, and especially for you, my beloved Creator, who has made me rich beyond belief with your blessings. Let my heart overflow with your grace as I celebrate the day. Please grant my Spirit the ability to be the bringer of gracious friendship and love to others, in your name. Let your grace speak through my words, my actions, and my thoughts and feelings this day, so that everyone I touch is surrounded by your love.

I thank you for the grace that you constantly bestow upon my path, in the form of supportive and kind people who are patient and generous with me, who share their talents, open their hearts, and extend their goodwill toward me so that my day unfolds with greater ease for me. I ask for your most holy grace to keep my Spirit centered and mindful of all the blessings I receive this day, taking nothing for granted, yet enjoying to the fullest everything that you offer me.

I thank you in advance for hearing my prayer this day and for the grace you shower upon my life, which allows my Spirit the opportunity to be a bearer of love and goodwill, and to bring more light to the dark corners of this world. I am grateful to you now and always.

Today's Mantra

Grant my Spirit the grace to bring more light to everything and everyone today.

Your Personal Blessing

Today, _____ (your name), I, your ever-loving Holy Mother-Father God, Creator of the Universe, and Source of all life, bless and fill your Spirit with my endless grace, so that you are filled with comfort and support with each breath you take.

I grace your mind with loving thoughts toward yourself so that you forgive all mistakes and appreciate your beautiful Spirit. I grace your Spirit with the ability to sit at the banquet of blessings I place before you this day so that you allow yourself to be filled with all that you can possibly absorb. I grace your Spirit with genuine love and affection for yourself, and the courage and confidence to be authentic and true with every person in your life. I grace your Spirit with abundant energy and life force so that you move with ease and fluidity each step of the day.

I grace your Spirit with exuberance and laughter that is shared with good friends, old and new, and with deep and profound companionship that fills your heart with peace. I bless and grace your Spirit with the fortitude to walk through all the losses and difficulties of the day with unwavering faith and dignity, and to release your pain through an easy flow of tears when necessary. I grace your Spirit with adequate time this day to enjoy the gifts of nature that surround you, and to sit and meditate with the elements so that you feel close to me, your Divine Creator and Source of all life.

I grace your conversation with humor and inspiration so that you forget the words before you speak of any negative communication, and replace those words with appreciative and lighthearted exchange that brings peace and calm to those with whom you engage. I bless your Spirit with the strength to face all painful moments in the eye, and yet remain openhearted and available to the love and support I offer you through these times, in the form of angels, both from heaven and on earth.

I grace your Spirit with a sense of meaning and purpose in all your actions, large and small, seen and unseen, knowing that all that is done in love fulfills your soul's purpose beyond all measure. I bless your Spirit with resilience through the ups and downs of this day, so that you ride them as a wave, so that you are on top of your experience, not buried under it and lost to yourself. I bless and grace your Spirit to shine through everything and bring a brilliance to all that you do so that you uplift and inspire even the most negative and jealous of onlookers to drop their judgments and opinions of you, and to instead join with you in fully loving each other and life this day.

And so it is in my name, the Holy Mother-Father God who created you and loves you unconditionally; the love, light, and healing of the Christ; and the power of the Holy Spirit that lives and moves in your being.

Message from Spirit

Generosity is grace working on conditions where unfairness exists. It is our ability to make what is unfair in the world better than the way we found it. This is our way of partaking in the process of creating heaven on earth.

Morning Prayer

Dear Holy Mother-Father God,

I pray for you to bestow your all-empowering grace upon me this day to be generous to others in all ways. Grace me with the mindfulness to be generous in my appreciation of others for the difference they make in my life. Allow me the generosity of mind to stop thinking only of myself and my point of view, and to verbally acknowledge those around me for the positive and meaningful difference they make in both my life and the world.

Allow me the generosity of Spirit to stop talking, even silently in my own mind, when others are speaking, and give them my full attention and willingness to hear and understand what they are saying, and value it enough to consider, even when their point of view differs greatly from my own. Grace my Spirit with the generosity of letting others go before me when I drive or travel through this day, rather than competitively push my way to the front just to be first. Allow me the graciousness to open doors for others and willingly step aside if they appear to need to get ahead of me in any way.

Grant me the grace to give generously of my time this day. Give me the impulse to pick up a phone and call a friend, and thank him or her for being in my life. Allow me to grace others with my full attention, listening as they speak, holding space and comforting them as they need comfort, laughing at their jokes even if I do not find them especially funny, and being fully with them rather than elsewhere in my mind.

Grace my Spirit with the ability to be generous as well. Allow me to pick up the tab for another's coffee, buy a friend lunch, or treat a loved one to a movie, flowers, or a small token of my love and appreciation for their presence in my life. Grace my Spirit with the integrity to pay an owed bill over buying myself an unnecessary trinket, and move me to donate to those in need around the world rather than spend the money on something for myself that I do not really need.

Grace my Spirit with the generosity to be a true neighbor and to help those next to me by mowing their lawn while I am in the process of mowing mine, or calling to ask if they need anything when I will be at the grocery store.

Allow me the generosity of Spirit to reach down and pick up the debris on the road and deposit it in the proper receptacles so that this planet is kept more beautiful and respected. Let me share my heart, by gracing everyone I meet with a genuine smile and full presence of mind to acknowledge them as important human beings whom I respect and treat with kindness.

Also grant me the grace to be generous with myself, especially in affording myself the time I need to move through this day at a proper pace, not rushed or in a state of emergency, but grounded in breath and traveling in a graceful, even-paced manner, free of stress or a false sense of urgency and drama.

I thank you in advance for hearing my prayer this day and for the grace that you shower upon my life, which allows my Spirit the opportunity to be a bearer of love and goodwill, and to bring more light to the dark corners of this world. I am grateful to you now and always.

Today's Mantra

Please grant my Spirit the grace to be generous this day.

Your Personal Blessing

Today, _____ (your name), I, your ever-loving Holy Mother-Father God, Creator of the Universe, and Source of all life, bless and fill your Spirit with my endless grace so that you feel as rich and abundant as I have created you to be.

I bless and grace your Spirit with the full awareness of your divine royalty so that you may freely and joyfully give where needed and yet never deplete your own resources, which are continually replenished by me, your Source of all. I bless and grace your Spirit with overflowing recognition of the Holy Spirit in all beings, acknowledging to them their wonderful presence so that they, too, may walk in confidence of abundance and blessings.

I bless and grace your Spirit with the ceaseless benevolence to allow others to come first, without disrespecting yourself. I grace your Spirit, _____ (your name), with the generosity to say yes with ease when asked by others for help, giving what truly serves without saving or rescuing at your own expense. I bless and grace your holy and Divine Spirit with the ability to easily share all that you have, whether it be time, money, patience, food, service, support, or anything else called for in need, with your brothers and sisters in life, especially with those with whom it is most difficult to share yet who clearly need it the most.

I bless and grace your Spirit this day with abundant protection, so that all unsafe, unpleasant, unloving energies in the energetic field around you are instantly deflected from your being, broken apart by angels, and transformed into pure light. I bless and grace your Spirit this day with abundant, lovely invitations; opportunities; and beautiful and generous surprises, delivered through many others but sent to you by me, your loving Mother-Father God, who delights in showering you with my love in all ways.

I bless and grace your Spirit to readily accept and receive all the goodness pouring forth to you from me this day without resistance, reluctance, hesitation, or fear, knowing in your heart the great pleasure it gives me to see you accept and delight in the endless bounty of life that I share with you. I bless and grace your Spirit with abundant kind words that pour forth from your lips, abundant creative and prosperous ideas that stimulate your mind, abundant relaxation that flows through your physical body, so that you experience this day as the best, most glorious day ever.

And so it is in my name, the Holy Mother-Father God who created you and loves you unconditionally; the love, light, and healing of the Christ; and the power of the Holy Spirit that lives and moves in your being.

Message from Spirit

Grace is the ability to accept the life you have been given by chance and then using your full set of skills to transform the conditions of that life to work at the highest level of possibility. Accept what you've been given and take the chance to make something wonderful happen with these conditions.

Morning Prayer

Dear Holy Mother-Father God,

I pray for you to bestow your all-empowering grace upon me this day so that I accept the life conditions I was born into, knowing that they are the perfect conditions in which to grow my soul and awaken my Divine authentic Self. Grant me the grace to intelligently strive to see and seize all opportunities laid before me in the conditions I received in this lifetime. Allow me the grace to kindly understand that my soul elected these conditions as the best incubator for its growth in this lifetime.

Grace my intelligence with the ability to recognize the good and the bad of my early childhood conditioning so that I take advantage and develop the good, while leaving behind the negative and unhealthy patterns that serve no empowering purpose. Grace me with objectivity and insight to see through my inherited negative patterns, and shed light upon them so that my authentic and loving self may consciously choose something better and healthier than simply mindlessly repeating what I observe in those unconscious people around me.

Grace me with the discipline and self-esteem to devote my time and efforts toward taking the circumstances of my life and turning them into positive and productive outcomes, for me and for my family on earth. Please afford me the grace to look at myself objectively and with honest assessment of where I am this day, and move me to release myself from nonproductive thoughts, behaviors, feelings, judgments, and resignations, so that I may move to higher ground no matter where I find myself in life.

Allow me the grace to seek balance above blind ambition so that I gracefully meet my needs, while not sacrificing the important qualities of life, such as family, friends, and time to enjoy this beautiful life you have afforded me. I ask for the grace to take personal responsibility for my response to the conditions of my life, knowing that I am responsible for no more than my reactions and choices, no matter what befalls me in life. Grace me with the ability to detach from my emotional investments and perspectives enough to see whether or not they are in my best interest and if they honor and support my most authentic Self.

Please grace my emotions with maturity and clarity so that I refrain from being overly sensitive, reactive, moody, or self-indulgent when life challenges me, and give me, in place of immature reactions, a mature and willing ability to respond to my life with acceptance, determination to improve and grow in love and kindness, and creative solutions to better myself, my relationships, and my conditions without complaint.

I thank you in advance for hearing my prayer this day and for the grace you have given me so that I can be a self-directed, self-loving, intelligent human being who lives and co-creates as your Divine and forever blessed child of light. I am grateful to you this day and always.

Today's Mantra

Please grant my Spirit the ability to be emotionally clear today.

Your Personal Blessing

Today, _____ (your name), I, your ever-loving Holy Mother-Father God, Creator of the Universe, and Source of all life, bless and fill your Spirit with my endless grace for you to appreciate your life, no matter the conditions in it.

I grace you with the wisdom to see the opportunities for your soul's growth in the circumstances you were born into and those that you are experiencing today. I grace you with the divine understanding that you are a co-creator with me of your world. I grace you with the empowering acceptance that the conditions of your world today are a mirror of the images and beliefs you've long held in your mind and that if the circumstances are not satisfying, you accept your error and begin to change them from the inside.

I bless and grace your Spirit with balanced emotions this day so that you refrain from indulging in self-pity or victimhood, but rather use your creative imagination and feeling body to choose and begin the steps to move toward something better. I grace you with mental clarity to see where you limit yourself with worn-out patterns and, in their place, activate the desire and ability to learn new ways to achieve your goals: ways that are grounded, consistent, and in harmony with your most authentic desires and highest visions.

I grace you with the integrity to use the talents I have given you this day, and share your gifts with the world freely. I grace you with the confidence to be in charge of your life, and accept full and joyful responsibility for creating the life you want.

I grace you this day with powerful and positive mentors, who will guide you out of confusion and self-limiting patterns, and introduce you to new and more effective ways to advance your body, mind, and soul toward the blinding and glorious light of your Divine Spirit. I bless and grace your Spirit with the discipline and patience to work on your highest goals with steadfast consistency so that you keep your eye on the goal while doing your fullest, on this day and all days, to achieve these goals.

I bless and grace your Spirit with determination to use all the circumstances of your life as fuel to advance toward your best possible expression of self so that you let none of them appear to be obstacles but, rather, see them as springboards to advance and strengthen your soul in every way.

I grace you with an honest and thorough work ethic so that you do your best this day, putting forth your best effort, fulfilling your commitments and agreements to the fullest, cutting no corners, and going beyond your ego's limitations to create and contribute to the full capacity of your abilities.

I bless and grace your Spirit to ask for help and support wherever you feel stuck or challenged, and to graciously receive, fully and quickly, all assistance offered without ego, pride, or defensiveness getting in the way. I grace your Spirit to end this day with a heart full of satisfaction and contentment, so that you know that you did your best and that whatever you did from your best will come back to you.

And so it is in my name, the Holy Mother-Father God who created you and loves you unconditionally; the love, light, and healing of the Christ; and the power of the Holy Spirit that lives and moves in your being.

Message from Spirit

Grace gives you the desire to go beyond just making your own life better. Grace directs your awareness and higher understanding toward helping others' lives work. It is the desire to change your focus from simply managing your own life but to helping the world become a more loving place. Grace gives us the ability to share everything we have with the world. It is the ability to be attached to nothing, and a willingness to share all that we have been given.

Morning Prayer

Dear Holy Mother-Father God,

I pray that you bestow your all-empowering grace upon me this day to redirect my attention from my own problems and concerns to the world around me and how to make it a better place. Grant me the grace to be extra kind and considerate to those I live with so that I go out of my way to keep our shared environment organized, placing my things where they belong and keeping the main living space that I share clear of my personal clutter and debris.

Grant me the grace to place a few calls or make a surprise visit to someone I know, who may be shut in or unable to get around as easily as I can, and allow me to gracefully lend a hand, such as by offering a ride to the store, cleaning up the person's front yard, or bringing in a few staple groceries.

Raise my awareness beyond myself with your grace so that I notice my environment, picking up the garbage on the street and placing it in a proper receptacle. Grace me with the opportunity to be of service to those who are in endless dire need in the world. Direct me to ways to contribute a few of my dollars to someone in a developing country so that that person may start his or her own business and become empowered.

Grace me with the generosity of heart to offer to stay longer at work to help a co-worker who needs to leave early and to do so with a pleasant attitude. Grant me the follow-through ability to go through my house and collect old eyeglasses, cell phones, and computers, and donate them to people or organizations that collect them for the needy. Give me the motivation to go through my closets and donate clothing that I no longer wear but that is perfectly good for those who are trying to get back to work and need clothing for job interviews.

Please God, grace me with the passion this day to be of endless and creative service to my fellow man and this planet in as many ways as possible. Show me, through your grace, ways that I can serve, ways that I have missed in the past. Flood me with your grace and use me this day to make this planet kinder, more loving, and more beautiful.

I thank you for hearing my prayer this day and for the grace that you have given me to be of service to humanity, now and always. I am grateful to you this day and always.

Today's Mantra

Please grace me with the ability to serve in all ways today.

Your Personal Blessing

Today, _____ (your name), I, your ever-loving Holy Mother-Father God, Creator of the Universe, and Source of all life, bless and fill your Spirit with my endless grace to show up in willing service to humanity and the planet.

I grace and bless your Spirit with the energy of a thousand people as you vigorously improve not only your environment, but also the environment of your fellow humans. I grace you with music in your heart as you clear and simplify your life, giving away all of the excess in your home, and spreading your wealth to others in the way of donations that help others feel more empowered.

I bless and grace you with the interest and patience to spend quality time with a child who sits in front of the television for too long so that you engage in meaningful conversation and show interest in his or her world. I grace and bless you with the power of Spirit to volunteer your time and energy to a meaningful cause today, one that will brighten the hearts of those who seem to have lost their light and their way.

I bless and grace your Spirit with the love to check on your neighbors and help those who are not as strong and energetic as you. I bless and grace your Spirit to share freely with others all that you have, and to spend your money on service to others rather than on consumption this day, happily and with joy. Today, by my decree, you will be graced with *the inspiration to reach out and support the children of my beautiful planet by offering your time and creative abilities to them, through donations, assistance, and encouragement.*

I grace and bless your Spirit to uplift all those you touch today, both at home and work, with your supportive and kind words, your extra efforts, and your generosity in all ways called for. I bless and grace your Spirit to smile and acknowledge the homeless people you encounter today and grace them with the dignity they have lost along the way, by looking them in the eye and smiling, and reminding them that you see the light in their hearts, even if they are temporarily blind to it. I bless and grace your Spirit with the nobility that you are, and use you to do my work, spreading love and light throughout this entire day. You are my beloved and blessed child, and I grace you with the power to be of humble and joyful service everywhere this day.

And so it is in my name, the Holy Mother-Father God who created you and loves you unconditionally; the love, light, and healing of the Christ; and by the power of the Holy Spirit that lives and moves in your being.

Message from Spirit

Grace takes away the limited breath of control and brings in the expanded and deeper breath of the Holy Spirit to move your life. Each deep breath expands our potential to receive God's grace. Pause for a moment. Tend your soul by staying with your experience rather than running from it. We avoid that which we need to feel in order to grow. Breathe in and attend the soul. Ask for the grace to attend to your soul's growth.

Morning Prayer

Dear Holy Mother-Father God,

I pray for you to bestow your all-empowering grace upon me this day to attend to the work of growing my soul. Give me the grace to sit with the discomfort of facing my negative patterns, shadows, and unenlightened behaviors with the understanding that I am the one creating these experiences, though on an unconscious level. Grace me with the courage to become aware of my self-sabotaging and limiting behaviors quickly so that I may pause before I mindlessly carry on and, with full breath and awareness, choose a more self-loving, conscious course that respects both my Spirit and that of others.

Grace

Grace me with the lucidity to recognize what serves my Spirit and is in integrity with my authentic Self, and what is not. Please allow your grace to lead me out of any victim-oriented response to life, replacing it with a fully conscious, dynamic, co-creative response that moves me toward the full expression of my true and Higher Self. Allow me the grace to stand in the face of the pain and disappointments that inevitably come with life this day, and not run from my emotional learning experience through mindless addictions or distractions that keep me from being fully present to my opportunities to grow.

Shine your grace upon the shadows of my soul, so that I may walk into the light of my Higher Self and stop hiding from my own glorious light. Grace me with breath, the reflection, and the willingness to take responsibility for myself and for creating my happiness this day. Lead me, with your loving grace, to the place where I am willing to own my power as a co-creator and begin to dedicate myself to using it fully and wisely, starting with this day.

Grace my mind with silence, so that I may stop trying to control life and, instead, begin to feel your presence and plan unfolding and guiding me toward the full realization of my holy self. I ask for your holy grace to help me listen to my Spirit over the negative and controlling grumblings of my severely limiting ego patterns, and to follow its wisdom toward higher and more creative, effective, fulfilling, and authentic ways of expressing my Spirit this day. Give me the grace to stay with pain and learn from it rather than deny or mask it with false pretense. Grace me to be present to my own transformational process this day.

I thank you this day and all days for the grace you give me to fearlessly mature and transform into the holy and divine co-creating Spirit you have created me to be.

Today's Mantra

Grace me with the courage to face my shadows this day.

Your Personal Blessing

Today, _____ (your name), I, your ever-loving Holy Mother-Father God, Creator of the Universe, and Source of all life, bless and fill your Spirit with my endless grace so that you awaken fully to your divine nature this day, and recognize and free yourself of your self-limiting habits and behaviors.

I bless and grace your Spirit to take over your choices and actions, and lead you directly into a powerful day of delightful and exciting co-creation of your heart's desire. I grace your Spirit with the power to recognize and shatter old patterns with your conscious and holy breath, and to walk free of addictive seductions and distractions. I grace and bless your Spirit to recognize what does not honor you and decisively walk away from it this day, without looking back.

I bless and grace your Spirit this day, _____ (your name), to awaken from your long unconscious sleep and take full command of your co-creative power by pausing to breathe in the holy breath of life before you speak, think, and act this day. I bless and grace your Spirit to flow with the Holy Spirit in you, which allows me to subdue and bind all lesser influences, thus rendering them powerless over you in every *way. I bless your thoughts to be reflections of your divine genius this day so that they carry with them healing, freedom, empowerment, and productivity all day.*

I bless and grace your emotions by liberating your nervous system from stuck, ancient, weakening, and fearful feelings that were meant to inform and move on at the time, but have been arrested in your body and are now taking away from your vitality. I grace you with the healing of body, mind, and soul this day, cleansing you of the shadows of erroneous and unconscious hidden beliefs and perceptions, born of your own and others' mistakes that limit and steal your divine power, and I replace them with a thunder bolt of self-awakening so that you remember your divine truth and walk free this day from your destructive illusions. I grace you with the courage and power to break free of your own internal monsters and start to live, this very day, as the Divine Being that I have created you to be.

And so it is in my name, the Holy Mother-Father God who created you and loves you unconditionally; the love, light, and healing of the Christ; and the power of the Holy Spirit that lives and moves in your being.

Message from Spirit

Grace removes fear, shame, regret, and guilt from one's personal energy field and vibration, and restores sanctity to life. It relieves us of the vibrational burdens and illusions we carry that prevent us from seeing our life circumstances from a place of the pure awareness of truth. Grace endows us with the necessary creative insight to transform all dramas and traumas in life into wholehearted adventures, and to simply embrace it and allow it to be just an experience.

Morning Prayer

Dear Holy Mother-Father God,

I pray to you this day to bestow your all-empowering grace upon me, to help me look upon my life experiences with neutrality and appreciation for all the great learning experiences my soul has had. Grace me with the ability to remove all harmful negative filters of judgment, shame, regret, and guilt that I project onto my soul experiences, preventing me from deriving the genuine value each one has brought to my life, and please instead inspire me to review my past with the interest and objectivity of a co-creator student who is here to learn all that is possible from each life experience and condition to grow my soul.

Grace

Bless and grace me with the clarity to recognize the negative repeating patterns that I create in my life with humor, yet to intelligently realize that now is the time that I choose to break free of such patterns as they come to my conscious attention, rather than naively and hypnotically believing that I must blindly suffer life as it is happening to me and that I can do nothing. Grace me with the ability to use my own power to observe my life, now and in the past, from a place free of distortion by my fearful ego or reactive emotions, granting me love and compassion for myself and all other players involved in my life's unfolding story.

Grace me with deep understanding in my heart and Spirit that all unfolds in your supreme perfection and that in Divine eyes there are no victims, only students of life, having experiences. Grace me, Dear Mother-Father God, with the awareness to see beyond my own temporary perceptions and emotional filters to the genuine opportunities each soul experience offers me, and keep me present with breath and attention to my power to choose, in each moment, a response to life that supports and respects my Spirit rather than that indulges me in the temptation to be victimized or make victims of people in my life.

I humbly ask you to grace me with the necessary detachment from each of my life's dramas to remember that they are in fact only dramas, good or bad, and that they will pass with time. Grace me with the ability to accept and embrace all facets of my life, both the beautiful and the scars of pain, with deep love and acceptance, knowing that each experience I have holds equal value in supporting the evolution of my soul to meet and merge with my Divine Spirit. Grace me with the ability to fully love my life this day.

I thank you in advance this day for hearing my prayer and granting me the grace to be a co-creative witness, freeing myself from victimhood responses and drama, learning with each experience to live more and more in holy power of the Spirit that I am.

Today's Mantra

Grant me the grace to experience life without judgment.

Your Personal Blessing

Today, _____ (your name), I, your ever-loving Holy Mother-Father God, Creator of the Universe, and Source of all life, bless and fill your Spirit with my endless grace to awaken you to your co-creative power and witness the story of your life free from all negative emotions or ego-based judgments.

I grace you with blessed and profound understanding of your soul plan this day, bringing with it complete appreciation and forgiveness for all your life experiences. With my grace, _____ (your name), I shake free from your bones, your memory, your nervous system, your thoughts, and your emotions all harsh, faulty, distorted, confused, and unloving perceptions, including shame, regret, guilt, and the need for punishment and revenge. These I replace with acceptance, awareness, and insight for the gifts each life drama has and will continue to bring to your soul.

I bless and grace your Spirit, through the power of my love, to review your life with delight, laughter, insight, understanding, forgiveness, and love. By my decree, as your Holy Mother-Father God, I free you this day of the fear of life, fear of others, fear of yourself, and fear of love. I bless and grace your most Holy Spirit, my divine child, with the indisputable recognition that life is a dream, created by you in order to learn how to wield the infinite power of creation that I have bestowed upon you.

With my grace, your perceptions are made clear this day, and your attention is solidly grounded fully in the present moment, free of enslavement to a guilty and regretful past. I free you to live the adventure of your life as I have always intended, restoring your sense of curiosity, wonder, and awe for the beauty of this planet and all the blessings pouring into your life and from you back to life. I bless and grace your Spirit with peace with the past, peace with others, and peace with yourself. Like water under the bridge, I grace you with the knowing that life unfolds and changes, and only memory clings to the past. I grace your Spirit to fully live, create, and enjoy this day with abandon.

And so it is in my name, the Holy Mother-Father God who created you and loves you unconditionally; the love, light, and healing of the Christ; and the power of the Holy Spirit that lives and moves in your being.

Message from Spirit

Grace allows us to transcend control and helps us stop trying to change life. It reminds us that there is a natural forward-moving force in all living beings that wants to return to its divine nature. We need not force it. Grace can only be received if your ego gives up control. Grace is a gift that the ego wants to reject. Realize the limitations of the ego and the fear it has of grace. To be able to receive grace, you must acknowledge the ego's limitations, which the ego never wants to do. So it is up to you whether or not you will allow grace into your life. Are you able to receive grace? Is your ego willing to give up control?

Morning Prayer

Dear Holy Mother-Father God,
I pray to you this day to bestow your all-empowering grace upon me so that I give up my futile efforts to control life and people, and surrender myself fully and with trust to your holy plan. Allow me, by your holy grace, to intuitively feel the force of nature moving in the direction of my highest good, and follow it without struggle, questioning, or resistance. Please grant me the ability to relax and breathe into your ever-present loving care,

and to open my heart fully to receive the gift of your loving grace.

Grace me with the courage to overcome my fear of your healing presence and to release my lingering doubt of your power to heal all things in my life. Grace me with the humility to recognize my own limitations, and to know that what I know is not all there is to know, thus opening my mind as a student learning to be a divine co-creative Spirit. Grace me with the common sense to get out of my own way this day, and open my heart and thinking to your inspiring influence.

I ask for the grace to stop pushing against life, trying to force it to go my way, and to instead completely surrender my will over to yours and allow Divine Will to move me this day. Let your grace take me to the best opportunities to be of service to this planet. Grace me with the awareness, sensitivity, interest in others, and love to be the best person, friend, parent, partner, employee, boss, or neighbor to those in my life I can be.

Grace me with the intelligence and honesty to stop manipulating others to cooperate with my hidden agendas and limited, self-serving plans, and allow me the trust and courage to stop imposing my fearful behaviors on unsuspecting others. I pray with my whole heart and soul to be open to receiving your grace this day. I know my limitations and restrictions, and without your grace, my life cannot flow in harmony with your generous plans for me. I am ready to receive your grace. Please show me the way.

I thank you in advance this day for hearing my prayer and granting me the grace to be easygoing, relaxed and receptive, spontaneous and guided by my intuition to follow the flow of your plan, learning more and more this day to trust in the power of Spirit that I am. I am grateful to you now and always.

Today's Mantra

Please grace me with spontaneity and the willingness to surrender to your wisdom over my own.

Your Personal Blessing

Today, _____ (your name), I, your everloving Holy Mother-Father God, Creator of the Universe, and Source of all life, bless and fill your Spirit with my endless grace so that you relax all your illusions and fears, and place yourself fully and without resistance into my care.

I bless and grace your Spirit with renewed energy and intuitive genius this day, moving you in the direction of answers and solutions before problems even present themselves to you. I grace and bless your Spirit with complete freedom from unnecessary, distracting, worrisome, and controlling thoughts so that you allow my guidance to fill your mind with inspired intelligence and decisive action in accordance with my plan.

I bless and grace your Spirit, _____ (your name), to flow this day with my brilliant and holy light all around you, lighting up every step of your day with my love. I bless and grace your Spirit with the power of attraction. Doors will open as you approach. People will offer loving assistance before you ask. By my grace, those who call will bear good news and offer you generous invitations.

I bless and grace you with full activation of your intuition, so that you know without question the next and best step as you flow with my angels and guardians throughout this day.

By my grace, I bless your Spirit to enter a state of complete, creative competence unlike ever before, bringing every effort you make to an entirely new level of excellence and excitement this day. I bless your Spirit with my grace, and I let it flow through your every cell. By my grace, I free your ego from all habitual, conscious, and unconscious attempts at control over others by known and hidden fearful agendas, leaving your heart and mind fully present, revitalized, and available to the power of the present moment.

I bless and grace your Spirit to create with ease this day. I bless and grace your Spirit to trust and accept your holy and royal nature as my beloved holy child, so that you know in your heart and embrace in your life the power I give you to create freely without the need to control or subdue any other person's freedom and energy. I bless and grace your Spirit with my power and protection, giving you full freedom to be authentic and empowered, free of the need to play "small" or try to overwhelm others, and able to flow through this day unencumbered by anything as you move through this blessed day.

And so it is in my name, the Holy Mother-Father God who created you and loves you unconditionally; the love, light, and healing of the Christ; and the power of the Holy Spirit that lives and moves in your being.

Message from Spirit

Grace guides us into the place of thanksgiving for all that we experience. It allows us to accept whatever happens with gratitude and unconditional nonresistance. We walk in grace when we choose to remain calm, with breath, and have an open heart in the face of all circumstances. Grace allows us to welcome life rather than run from it. This is a gift from God.

Morning Prayer

Dear Holy Mother-Father God,

I pray to you this day to bestow your all-empowering grace upon my Spirit, to open my heart so that I fully accept all that comes my way this day, knowing that all experiences open doors to higher learning and greater empowerment if only I am willing to see this truth.

Bless and grace my Spirit with the mindfulness to breathe deeply and remain centered today, even if the experiences I meet cause me stress or challenge me to make an unexpected change. Give my Spirit the grace to speak my truth in a clear and calm manner, without blame or guilt, and to ask clearly for what I want from others, while still being willing to have my request denied.

Grant me the grace to remember and act as an adult who is fully in charge of my life experience, recalling that I have the power to choose how I respond to all that unfolds before me this day. Grace me with the self-control to breathe and check in with my Spirit before I do respond this day so that I behave in alignment with my Higher Self and my true nature in present time. Grace my Spirit with the ability to feel my emotions fully and learn from them, rather than act them out in a negative way or try to hide them in an attempt to distance myself from my feelings.

Grace my Spirit, Divine Creator, with the power to turn every situation I meet into an empowered occasion for me to co-create what I truly envision for my life. Grace and bless my Spirit with objectivity and detachment this day, so that I can accept what unfolds before me without taking responsibility for what is not mine, while responding appropriately to what is.

Grace and bless my Spirit with overwhelming gratitude for all the hidden gifts that come with experience, even if the gift is that of giving me the occasion to be mature and grounded this day, responding to life without adding my own drama. Grace my Spirit with the ability to participate fully in this day, observing and learning from everything and everyone, while not absorbing the negative energy swirling around me and internalizing it as my own. Grace my Spirit by allowing me to welcome it into a healthy, happy home in my body, removing from my nervous system residual negative energy held there from the past that may disturb my peaceful vibrations.

I thank you in advance for hearing my prayer and granting me the grace to respond to this day with maturity, gratitude, and detachment, creating what I want with what I am given without drama or unnecessary emotional upset. I am grateful to you now and always.

Today's Mantra

Please grace my Spirit with detachment, self-control, and inner peace this day.

Your Personal Blessing

Today, _____ (your name), I, your ever-loving Holy Mother-Father God, Creator of the Universe, and Source of all life, bless and fill your Spirit with my endless grace so that you meet this day with detachment, objectivity, quick ability to learn, and the empowerment of a true and divine co-creator, as you are designed by me to be.

I grace and bless your Spirit this day to engage fully in all that unfolds while I stand before you and deflect all drama and needless confusion swirling around from your being, keeping you calm and grounded, and your Holy Spirit undisturbed by life's events. I grace and bless your Spirit to oversee all the day's events as the true master co-creator that you are, observing your own masterpiece of this day with interest and affection. I bless and grace your Spirit to quickly take from each experience the best that this day has to offer, and I have my angels sweep in and remove you from the unnecessary wear and tear of drama, before you ever feel the least ripple of dissonance touching your aura.

I grace and bless your Spirit to rise above the fray of struggling with others, so that you glide through this day with absolute ease and joy. By my decree and through the power of my grace, your Spirit will stand in full command of the day, welcoming all that I bring you with an open and accepting heart, fearless and confident and ready to accept the gifts placed before you with eagerness. I grace and bless your

Spirit so that you walk freely in this day, with the past fallen to the wayside and your mind fully present and ready to meet the moment.

By my grace, your Spirit will shine brightly this day, enlightening the dull imaginations of those you meet who have forgotten their divine heritage, and calling them back to life. I grace your Spirit with the power to heal those who habitually miss the glorious world right before their eyes, by simply witnessing the joy and enthusiasm you hold for this holy and sanctified day. By my grace, all those who stand in your presence this day will instantly feel more energy, clarity, freedom, and gratitude for the gift of life than ever before. I grace and bless your Spirit to be my holy ambassador this day so that you cast light and love, peace and calm, gratitude and appreciation wherever you go.

And so it is in my name, the Holy Mother-Father God who created you and loves you unconditionally; the love, light, and healing of the Christ; and the power of the Holy Spirit that lives and moves in your being.

Message from Spirit

We can invoke the presence of grace through humble prayer. As we pray for ourselves, we must also remember to include others in our prayers as well. Grace makes us aware that we are all part of one spiritual body and that our prayers for others heal the one family of humanity.

Morning Prayer

Dear Holy Mother-Father God,

I pray to you with all my heart and soul this day to bestow your all-empowering grace upon my beloved human family that they may experience a day of personal peace and awakening to the holiness within.

Please infuse my family members with your holy grace, so that each one faces his or her personal challenges with more confidence and faith to overcome these obstacles quickly and without unnecessary pain. I ask you to shed your grace upon the people in this world who have suffered losses due to the extreme changes being visited upon this planet in these times. Grace those who have lost loved ones, homes, health, and security as a result of earthly disruptions due to no personal fault of their own. Please grace those who work to salvage others from these extreme losses with the fortitude and strength to do such devastatingly harsh and painful work for the sake of the rest of us.

I humbly ask that you shine your holy power and grace upon the Spirits of those who suffer from depression and loss of faith in these times, and I ask for grace for those who live and work with such dispirited souls, to keep them from feeling responsible for or drained by the suffering of others. I ask you to send your holy and all-powerful grace to those who are cast in battles within their own hearts, within their close personal relationships, within their neighborhoods, cities, and countries, that they feel able to put down their weapons and embrace peace for themselves and others.

I humbly pray for your grace to uplift the hearts and Spirits of those who teach our children, that they may remember the value and importance of their contributions on a soul level, and feel appreciated and worthwhile, so that they continue to do their loving service, which is so greatly needed in these times. I ask for grace upon those who have lost their health and energy, that they are able to call their Spirits back home to their bodies once again and find the divine spark of life you have given them to help restore them to full vitality according to your holy plan.

And please, Holy Mother-Father God, Source of all life, please grace my Spirit with the opportunity to be an ambassador of your holy grace, that I may be of genuine assistance to those in need without grandiosity or ego, being grateful to serve and doing so quietly, knowing that it is your gift to me to be able to be an agent of your holy grace upon this planet this day.

I thank you in advance this day for hearing my prayer and granting my human family the grace to experience this day with strength, compassion, creativity, and resilience, no matter what is now unfolding or has already unfolded. I am grateful to you now and always.

Today's Mantra

Holy Mother-Father God, please grace me with resilience and strength this day.

Your Personal Blessing

Today, _____ (your name), I, your everloving Holy Mother-Father God, Creator of the Universe, and Source of all life, bless and fill your Spirit with my endless grace by hearing your prayer and fulfilling your request.

I bless and grace your Spirit to serve, in my name, all those in need of my divine support today, and to do so without a drain on your own personal energy or reserves. I grace and bless your Spirit to uplift your family, friends, and co-workers with kind and inspiring words, while you remain free from involvement in any negative patterns and vicious cycles of self-undoing. I bless and grace your most Holy Spirit with the intuition and creativity to infuse others with a deep sense of self-love and appreciation for their Holy Spirit within, erasing from their memory this day all wrongly learned distortions that would interfere with their ability to freely love and take joy in their most wonderful and divine nature.

I bless and grace your Spirit to instill an inner calm and sense of peace in those around you who fruitlessly battle for power and control, causing them to lay down their weapons of struggle this day and to find power instead in their personal connection to me, the Source of all life. I bless and grace your Spirit with the power to call back the fragmented pieces of those whose Spirit has been scattered and lost in the dramas of their past human experience, and to do so by simply being in your loving vibration. I grace and bless your Spirit to serve as teacher in my name this day, activating in others all around you the deep knowledge that they are beautiful, empowered, creative, and holy beings, infinitely loved now and always.

I bless and grace your Spirit with healing energy this day, relieving those in your presence of stress and suffering by uplifting their Holy Spirits with your compassion and understanding. I bless and grace your Holy Spirit to bring smiles and laughter where there are clouds of confusion and dark walls of fear. I bless and grace your Spirit to distract others from their suffering with your humor and kindness, inspired by me, your divine, loving Source of all creation, so that in my name, you help answer prayers, simply by your gentle presence and sanctified Spirit. I bless and grace your Spirit to work in my name, free from stress, protected from the dark pain and suffering of others, immune to drama and fatigue, and filled with laughter and light throughout this day.

And so it is in my name, the Holy Mother-Father God who created you and loves you unconditionally; the love, light, and healing of the Christ; and the power of the Holy Spirit that lives and moves in your being.

Message from Spirit

Grace reveals the healing, necessary energy to restore us to wholeness. It brings awareness to those aspects of ourselves that are out of alignment with the authentic Higher Self. Grace brings back parts of ourselves that we have lost in the journey of life. Grace restores courage. Grace restores strength. Grace restores our ability to be utterly honest with ourselves and others. Grace gives us the ability to stand up for what is right and good. Grace gives us the graciousness to live in our true Spirit without a need to impose our perceptions on others. Grace restores us to God's Divine perfection.

Morning Prayer

Dear Holy Mother-Father God,

I pray to you this day to bestow your all-empowering grace upon my Spirit to recognize and change those behaviors and choices that do not reflect who I authentically am and desire to be.

Grace my Spirit with the courage to speak up and voice my genuine self, and to take full responsibility for sharing my truth. Please remove from my actions those behaviors that are weak and victim oriented, that blame others, give away my power, or sidestep the work of living a life of integrity and truth. Please, Holy Mother-Father

God, grace my Spirit with the willingness to look at my own pain with the intention to learn, knowing that it is the result of important lessons, nothing more or less.

Allow me, by your most holy grace, to see through my own veils of distortion and to release my own stories and excuses for not living as the co-creator I am designed to be. Grace me with the courage to choose, with self-love over selfishness, the path of my true nature this day. Grace me with the strength to walk away from interactions and habits that reflect something other than my deepest and most genuine self. Grant me the grace to be clear and forthright, and to speak my heart without drama, blame, or judgment, but rather with a clear resolve to do what is necessary to move toward a deeper alignment with my heart and Spirit.

Allow my Spirit the grace to be the best possible mature, loving self that I can be today without being fearful of others' opinions, reactions, or rejections, including those of people closest to me. I pray for the grace to hear feedback from others without defense or resentment, giving all that comes my way honest consideration, knowing that in all of it, there is a kernel of truth, even if I do not want to look at it.

Grace me with the ability to recognize that the world serves as an honest and unwavering mirror of truth, and all that I experience in others is sourced in my choices and behaviors, not the other way around. Grace my Spirit with the dignity to take criticism without collapsing into shame or capitulating into approval seeking, allowing me to separate truth from manipulation, working with truth and ignoring manipulation. Grace my Spirit with the ability to learn all that I possibly can this day to become an even more capable and empowered divine co-creator.

I thank you in advance this day for hearing my prayer and granting my Spirit the ability to override all ego deflections or maneuvers that would keep me small or enslaved to my own illusions and sense of victim-hood. I thank you in advance this day for hearing my prayer and granting my Spirit the grace to face my weaknesses and move into the strength and power of my true divine nature. I am grateful to you now and always.

Today's Mantra

Please give me the grace to face and move beyond my weaknesses and fears.

Your Personal Blessing

Today, _____ (your name), I, your ever-loving Holy Mother-Father God, Creator of the Universe, and Source of all life, bless and fill your Spirit with my endless grace to see the truth of your holy nature and fully embody your divine presence.

I grace and bless your Spirit to fully embody and override your human limitations this day, freeing you from the fear of your own magnificence as my divine and holy child. I bless and grace your Spirit to reach out and call home all fragmented aspects of your soul, retrieve all your lost and ignored gifts and talents, resurrect your divine sense of purpose, and recall all power that you have surrendered over to others now and in all past life experiences, restoring you to wholeness as I have created you.

Grace

I bless and grace your Spirit to tower over and suppress all negative energies and influences, so that you rise above and walk free of all potential soul disturbances, and move with ease and by my grace through all seeming obstacles and barriers this day. I bless and grace your Spirit, _____ (your name), with humility of ego to bow to the power of the Divine Spirit within you and let your holy inner light shine on all shadows and veils that block or obstruct your authentic and holy essence.

I bless and grace your Spirit with the wisdom to immediately recognize the value of all that the Universe mirrors back to you in the form of feedback, criticism, and the frustrating behavior of others, to quickly learn from these reflections and then release them just as quickly, so that the lessons need not return again. I bless and grace your Spirit with the joy of empowered creativity, so that you experience great satisfaction this day with the ability to manifest your dreams and goals with uncomplicated ease and swiftness.

I bless and grace your beloved Spirit with cheerful courage and glorious vitality as you reclaim yourself fully as an authentic and divine child of mine. I bless and grace your Spirit to guide your ascending soul to my light this day, to leave behind all fearful and confused attachment to false sources of power, drawing all power only from me, your Holy Mother-Father God, Source of all life and creation.

By my grace you will walk this day with impeccable integrity and wholeness of soul, humility, and God-like presence, gaining respect and affection wherever you go. I grace and bless your Spirit with elegance and dignity, to peacefully attract cooperation and support from those who would otherwise oppose you. I bless and grace your Spirit with my commanding presence, which is loving, unwavering, and all powerful. Where you walk this day, by my grace, my angels will walk before you and bless and open your way.

And so it is in my name, the Holy Mother-Father God who created you and loves you unconditionally; the love, light, and healing of the Christ; and the power of the Holy Spirit that lives and moves in your being.

❦

Message from Spirit

Grace opens your heart and allows you to keep it open, even if you have been so injured and wounded that you have many reasons to close it. Grace gives you the strength to fearlessly love without condition. Grace is the hand of God in yours, as you walk together and work together, with God in the lead, bringing light and love wherever you go and leaving love in the heart of every person you touch.

Morning Prayer

Dear Holy Mother-Father God,
I pray to you to bestow your all-empowering grace upon my Spirit to keep my heart open and receptive this day, so that I drop all defenses and deflections that would attempt to control or push life away. Please bless my Spirit with your most holy grace to choose love over fear toward others in my life, and help me to be willing to release and surrender the wounds of my past for the power of life and love available to me today.

Grace my Spirit with the ability to love myself unconditionally, releasing my resentments and angers, and to help me breathe through my negative emotional reactions and desires for revenge or punishment. Grace me with the ability to feel the raw, intense, and even childish emotions of my wounded inner self, and bring the light of love, understanding, maturity, and compassion to those injured places within me so that they can heal, rather than have me continue to cover them over with false bravado and masked hardness.

I pray for your holy grace this day so that I feel your presence and love in my heart and, in it, find the ability to let go of my hurt and relax into your protection and support in its place. Grace my Spirit, most Holy Mother-Father God, with the ability to override the defended intensity of my fragile and reactive inner child and overbearing ego, and give me the ability to surrender my illusion of control over to your most holy plan for me. Fill my heart with the grace of your understanding and acceptance of all beings, especially those who have caused me the greatest pain and deepest wounding. Grace me with the ability to let go of my wounded perceptions and see that there is only learning, however painful, and to recognize how my every life experience has been my blessing.

I humbly ask for the grace to see my own self-undoing, my own self-sabotage, my own vicious cycles, my own "setups" that leave me feeling abandoned time and again. Grace me with the courage and power to stop my unconscious behaviors, to breathe before I respond and do something new and empowering instead. Grace me with the ability to be a student of light and learn how to live as an empowered co-creative being. Please, through your most Holy Grace, let me see through my own veils of distortion and step through them into my true divine nature.

I thank you in advance this day for hearing my prayer and granting my Spirit the grace to grow into the

Divine Being that I am designed to be. I am grateful to you now and always.

Today's Mantra

Please grace me with the strength and courage to grow beyond my own self-undoing this day.

Your Personal Blessing

Today, _____ (your name), I, your ever-loving Holy Mother-Father God, Creator of the Universe, and Source of all life, bless and fill your Spirit with my endless grace so that you stand tall in your power and see through your deep, human, wounded state to find the gift that each painful experience bears for you. I bless and grace your Spirit to breathe in the love that I have for you and to realize beyond any doubt or resistance of ego how treasured and loved you are at all times.

I bless and grace your Spirit to awaken to the empowered light within you and to cast that light upon all hidden or disguised shadows or patterns that prevent you from experiencing the love that I, your Mother-Father God, shine upon you at all times, or that prevent you from seeing the benevolence and love the Universe has for you now and forever. I bless and grace your Spirit to break free from all vicious self-undoing habits or behaviors that thrive on drama and try to cast away or deflect love.

Wherever you walk this day, _____ (your name), all attraction to drama subsides and disappears, and the light of love overwhelms all of your senses and guides your choices. I bless and grace your holy and Divine Spirit with deep intuition and the inner truth to steer away from all that belittles your sense of power, and I grace you to walk with the confidence and receptivity of an advanced student of consciousness. I bless and grace your Spirit with emotional self-control that allows you to feel the intensity of your emotions without irrationally acting on them in a loveless and or victim-oriented manner.

By my divine decree, I invoke my angel guardians to scatter your conscious and unconscious detractors, both internal and external, that prevent you from seeing and using the power of your Spirit to create this day as you choose, and I open the way for you to see, understand, heal, and release all wounds from the past that take you away from the power of the moment.

I bless you with the consciousness of an empowered creator, so that you breathe fully and decisively into this day exactly what experiences you desire to have, while releasing those deadened experiences from years and even lives before, and transforming them into fuel for better and happier creations this day. I bless and grace your Spirit with the profound knowing that you are safe and free to open your heart without fear or injury, and guide you to do so more and more with each breath you take this day.

And so it is in my name, the Holy Mother-Father God who created you and loves you unconditionally; the love, light, and healing of the Christ; and the power of the Holy Spirit that lives and moves in your being.

❧ ❖ ❧

Message from Spirit

Grace finds us when we accept life as it unfolds, even though, at times, we do not like what is happening. Grace gives us the wisdom to cease arguing with God, demanding that life be what we want and not the way it is, and helps us find the gifts in what is so. Grace gives us the intelligence to trust that all that is happening does ultimately serve a higher good, even though it may be hidden or deeply buried underneath a pile of rubble, in the form of loss, devastation, disappointment, and disease. Grace trusts God over our own perceptions.

Morning Prayer

Dear Holy Mother-Father God,

I pray to you to bestow your all-empowering grace upon my Spirit this day so that I admit my ego-based arrogance and rejection of you, and acknowledge the holy power you bestow upon me to co-create my life. Please grace me with the humility to cease arguing with life and begin taking responsibility for the life I am given and the way I have chosen to respond to it. I humbly ask for your most loving grace to help me to consciously recognize my creative role in all that I experience, and to view my life with the fresh eyes of a student who is learning how to use my power correctly.

Grace me, most Holy Mother-Father God, with acceptance of my mortality and the inevitable loss and temporary nature of all that comes with being in human form today. Grace me to use my intelligence to serve rather than fight my Spirit, and to allow my intellect and intuition to work together to give me a balanced and grounded approach to my life as it unfolds before me. Please, most Holy Mother-Father God, grace me with strength of Spirit to rise from the ashes of all that is collapsing or changing in my life right now: all sickness, disappointment, struggles, and endings, and grace me to move on with renewed faith and acceptance of life as it is.

Above all, most holy Creator, grace me with the ability to use my sensory perceptions correctly, and to trust and act on my deepest inner knowing without hesitation or question. I humbly ask for your grace to help me to go with the flow of your divine plan and to stop insisting on my own plan. Assist me so that I do not fret, pout, withhold from others, shut my heart down, act in passive-aggressive ways, behave manipulatively, or try to emotionally coerce others to take responsibility for my happiness or desires. Grant me the grace to act as an empowered, divine, and loving being in my interactions this day. Keep my internal conversations honest and responsible so that I may succeed in my relationships and in my creative efforts today.

I thank you in advance this day for hearing my prayer and granting my Spirit the grace to grow into the Divine Being that I am designed to be. I am grateful to you, now and always.

Today's Mantra

Please grant me the grace to recognize and use my power correctly this day.

Your Personal Blessing

Today, _____ (your name), I, your ever-loving Holy Mother-Father God, Creator of the Universe, and Source of all life, bless and fill your Spirit with my endless grace so that you silence your ego and listen to your heart, guided by my love and direction, and aligned with your highest empowerment.

I bless and grace your most Divine and Holy Spirit with the eager, open heart and mind of a student in the most exciting classroom of your soul's history. I bless and grace your Spirit with deep comprehension of your true and divine nature, and with the inspiration to create a more beautiful world today than ever before. I grace and bless your thoughts so that they are free of any but the most enlightened and supportive ideas. I bless and grace your emotions with the most balanced and calming of feelings so that they serve to move thought into the reality of the life experiences you choose this day. I bless and grace your Spirit to create with your words so that as you speak this day, so will you attract into being what you claim for yourself.

I grace you, _____ (your name), with the power to hear your intuition without effort and follow without interruption the plan of your Higher Self. I grace you with the power of attraction in all matter of focus. As you will it, you will attract immediate support for your intentions and goals. Doors will open as you approach. People will say *yes as you make requests. Obstacles will fall to the wayside before you meet them on your path. I grace and bless your Spirit to enter the divine flow of the Universe, experiencing abundance and richness as never before. By my decree, you will understand this day that, as my holy child, all belongs to you. Your Spirit will be free of competition, anxiety, struggle, and drama, as you experience the power that you inherently have at your disposal.*

I bless and grace your Spirit to be filled this day with a keen sense of purpose and meaning in your life, and calm inner knowledge that all is well now and forever. I grace and bless your Spirit with deep relaxation and trust in the moment this day, freeing you of the distraction of past and future.

And so it is in my name, the Holy Mother-Father God who created you and loves you unconditionally; the love, light, and healing of the Christ; and the power of the Holy Spirit that lives and moves in your being.

Message from Spirit

Grace removes all obstacles on your path. Grace removes the fear that you are alone and abandoned. Grace removes the fear that you are separate from God. Grace gives you the world. Grace gives you the Universe.

Morning Prayer

Dear Holy Mother-Father God,

I pray to you to bestow your all-empowering grace upon my Spirit this day, to help me release and let go of my need to suffer. Grace me with the ability to apologize for my hurtful words and behaviors and, to the best of my ability, make amends this day to those I have harmed. Please grace my Spirit with ease as I draw all my needs—body, mind, and soul—from your eternal well of Divine Source, knowing that there is no end to what I can access from your loving waters of life and that I therefore have nothing to fear.

Grace me with good company in the form of supportive and kind people who encourage the best in me, who are patient and generous with me, sharing their talents, opening their hearts, extending their goodwill toward me, and holding up strong and healthy boundaries, so that my day unfolds with greater ease. Lead me, with your loving grace, to own my power as a co-creator and dedicate myself to using it fully and wisely, starting with this day.

Let me acknowledge and embrace the unlimited love and support you make available to me this day, and use it to create a more beautiful world. I ask for the grace to serve your most holy plan in everything I do this day. I ask for your Holy Grace to keep me mindful of my true place in the Universe as your holy and beloved child and servant, and to stay faithful to my inner and outer work as a Spiritual light worker, who is here to bring more love and peace to this beautiful and blessed planet this day.

Please, Holy Mother-Father God, bestow your holy grace upon me this day so that I may be an agent of your never-ending love and peace on this beautiful and blessed planet. I thank you in advance this day for hearing my prayer and granting my Spirit the grace to experience this day as your holy child of the Universe. I am grateful to you now and always.

Today's Mantra

Please grant me the grace to feel your loving presence in my heart today.

Your Personal Blessing

Today, _____ (your name), I, your ever-loving Holy Mother-Father God, Creator of the Universe, and Source of all life, bless and fill your Spirit with my Holy Grace so that you confidently and fearlessly walk hand in hand with me, your loving Creator, as your closet companion and most loving support, this and every day. I bless and fill your Spirit with my grace so that you fearlessly trust in the goodness of this world and the people in it, and speak up and share positive feedback and support to all those with whom you are blessed to interact this day. I bless and fill your Spirit with my grace so that you take charge of your ego and train it to turn to me for guidance, rather than fight others and run away from my light and love.

I bless and grace your Spirit this day with abundant protection so that all unsafe, unpleasant, unloving energies in the energetic field around you are instantly deflected from your being, and broken apart by angels and transformed into pure light. I bless and grace your Spirit this day with abundant, lovely invitations, opportunities, and beautiful and generous surprises, delivered through many others but sent to you by me, your loving Mother-Father God, who delights in showering you with my love in all ways. I grace and bless your Spirit to shed all filters that dare to rob you of the full experience of life this day, as my holy guardian angels banish from your path and from your thoughts any and all energetic detractors of life or purveyors of victimhood.

I bless and grace your Spirit to move through this day enthusiastically and with great appreciation for all my blessings to you. I bless and fill your Spirit with my holy and unceasing, loving grace this day as I enlighten your thoughts with inspiration, vision, intuition, and insight, shedding light on your path each step of the way. I bless and fill your Spirit with my grace so that you will feel uplifted by the beauty of nature surrounding you, and I instill in you the desire to shine upon the world the beauty that I have placed in your heart. I bless and flood your Spirit with such abundance of healing grace that your ego happily surrenders fully now and forever to your Spirit. I bless you with the power and beauty of the Universe.

And so it is in my name, the Holy Mother-Father God who created you and loves you unconditionally; the love, light, and healing of the Christ; and the power of the Holy Spirit that lives and moves in your being.

GUIDANCE

Message from Spirit

Intuitive guidance does not necessarily communicate with us silently. In fact, intuition rarely comes to our attention this way. More often, it comes to our attention by way of subtle energy and vibration moving through time and space until it finally touches us in some subtle physical way: a slight rumble in the belly, a flush across the forehead, a tightening in the chest. Once we perceive this vibration, we must then learn to interpret this energy such that it informs our way. The intellect cannot translate subtle energy and vibration, and so discards it as meaningless. Only the heart understands the language of vibration. The heart decodes subtle vibration beautifully, as this is the language of the heart. If you listen to the heart, you will understand what all subtle guidance is conveying.

Morning Affirmation

My Divine and Holy Spirit expresses to me through all of my earthly senses in the form of subtle inner guidance. I am finely tuned to this gentle force of holy wisdom, and I pay attention to every subtle way in which it serves to communicate with me. I experience this holy force of inner guidance with each heartbeat pulsing through my body. I experience it moving me through life with each breath I take. I recognize my inner guidance communicating with me in every gentle flutter in my stomach, every sudden tickle in my throat, every single hair raising on the back of my neck and more.

I understand that the Holy Spirit within contacts my mind through the power of vibration, and therefore I trust my vibes as meaningful messages from my Divine Self. I am in intimate and accepting contact with the force and power of my Divine Self as my personal guidance system in every moment of this day. My Divine Guidance leads my life, and I follow in absolutely cooperative and peaceful surrender. And so it is.

Today's Mantra

I trust my vibes.

Your Personal Blessing

_____ (your name here), let peace reign in your heart this day, for you are forever blessed and held in the light and love of your ever-loving Holy Mother-Father God.

Your Divine Spirit is in perfect charge of your life and is guiding you in every moment. You are my Holy and blessed child, sent forth by my decree. You are a precious and beloved treasure, loved, protected, and watched over by me with every breath you take this day. Quiet your thoughts and feel the force of my holy light of Spirit guiding your way.

Turn your attention to the holy force living inside your heart, and surrender all personal distraction and worry over your safety to the Holy Spirit, who is overseeing your every *step with a powerful, unceasing force of protection. I bless you. I love you. I watch over you as a priceless and beautiful creation of heaven. Listen, _____ (your name), to all subtle nuances and whispered clues from heaven this day. They are your light. They show the way. They shower you with blessings. I bless your every breath with Divine Guidance this day. You will see the light and truth in all things. You will feel my peace.*

And so it is in my name, the Holy Mother-Father God who created you and loves you unconditionally; the love, light, and healing of the Christ; and the power of the Holy Spirit that lives and moves in your being.

Message from Spirit

The great *aha* in consciousness that occurs when we are awakening to the dynamic force of inner guidance is that we begin to realize that there is a benevolent and loving power at work beyond our ego that wants to assist us in realizing a deeper meaning, purpose, and sense of wholeness in our lives. The more we pay attention to this guidance, the more we notice visible, striking, almost magical incidents of sudden support working for our benefit. This powerful force is the Holy Spirit reaching toward us in love. And it makes life wonderful indeed!

Morning Affirmation

I delight in knowing, without any doubt, that the Universe is lovingly designed to support me, guide me, lead me, and assist me in every way to experience the deepest meaning and highest purpose in my life this day. I walk in the center of holiness at every moment. I am never outside of God. I am forever cradled in God. I recognize all synchronicities, all "chance" encounters, and *aha* moments that arise this day to be absolute evidence and confirmation of my loving Holy Mother-Father God's presence watching over me. I see the humor and lightness of play in these delightful, intuitive, and synchronistic way that the Universe reaches out to me. I cannot fail. I am guaranteed to succeed in being my most illuminated self this day. I am aware and enjoy the unfolding of my Divine Self in the ever-loving light of God.

Today's Mantra

I cannot fail. I only learn.

Your Personal Blessing

This day showers blessings upon you, _____ (your name), as the Universe takes joy in delighting your path with magical moments and playful assistance.

I, Your Holy Mother-Father God, bless you this day with invisible help from every direction. Light will shine on your path as well as in your heart. It will fall from the lips of strangers as well as in the loving words of most intimate beloveds. As you walk in the light and love of your Creator this day, the path will easily and effortlessly unfold. People will go out of their way to open doors for you, _____ (your name). Kind hands will reach out spontaneously with help and generosity. Sudden openings will occur where there once were obstacles. Conversations will unfold naturally that will point you toward the next step with ease. Confusion will give way to clarity, and your heart will sing with joy as you experience God's love and support all around you.

Everywhere you turn, the Universe will provide another clue for you to playfully uncover in fulfilling your next goal. Play the game with the Universe of finding your authentic Spirit, as if you were a child playing hide-and-seek, knowing that your loving light partner in God wants you to not only win the game, but also enjoy the game of your life this day with all your heart. I bless you this day with safety, protection, friendship, support, opportunity, and adequate means for every need, physical, mental, and emotional. Relax and walk through this day in peace. You cannot fail.

And so it is in my name, the Holy Mother-Father God who created you and loves you unconditionally; the love, light, and healing of the Christ; and the power of the Holy Spirit that lives and moves in your being.

Message from Spirit

Inner guidance is most often so subtly conveyed to the conscious mind that one must be on the constant lookout for it in order not to miss it. The best way to do this is to recognize inner guidance as a natural and even essential part of your life, and expect it to be present. Inner wisdom may reveal itself at any moment. It is up to you to notice it. There is no predictable time or way in which these energies are felt, but with awareness you will recognize its presence and embrace it with an open heart and mind every time.

To benefit from the power of inner guidance, you must do far more than simply recognize it when it does present itself, however. You must embrace such inner guidance as essential to your authentic self and trust what you feel enough to let it move you to experience its gift. The moment to move with intuition is now. To pause, hesitate, or resist such Divine influence is to lose your moment and its gifts.

Morning Affirmation

I am calm and clear throughout this day. I notice all subtle energy hidden in each moment, and I understand all as important messages sent by my Divine Higher Spirit to keep me safe, grounded, protected, and informed at the highest level. I am fully aware of each energetic signal, each subtle vibration sent my way. My conscious and subconscious minds register this energy fully. No energetic or intuitive message is ever ignored, missed, or lost. My thinking mind and my physical body instantly and completely surrender influence and control over my being to my higher subtle awareness, and follow its direction without hesitation or reserve. I place full control of my life in the care, guidance, and influence of my Holy Spirit at all times. So it is and will be.

Today's Mantra

I am calm.

Your Personal Blessing

_____ (your name), enter this day *with a light and joyful heart, as I, your Holy Mother-Father God, bless you with a clear mind; a calm, grounded physical body; and an attentive and fully aware Holy Spirit.*

Breathe deep and relax your thinking mind into the knowing that I, your Holy Mother-Father God, Creator, and Source of your Being, love and delight in your existence, and so watch over your every step with constant diligence and loving care. Be calm and release all tension in your physical body as I bless you with safety. I bless you with a clear and sharp sensory awareness that scrutinizes your every moment and sheds a powerful and loving light on all shadows, all that is hidden, and all that is contrary to your highest good, well in advance of any danger.

*I bless your Spirit with quiet attention, _____
(your name). I bless your heart with open receptivity to the
living influence of Divine Spirit that moves you along your
path. I bless you with flexibility of mind and body so that
as the holy force of guidance presents itself, you flow easily
with its grace. I, the Holy Mother-Father God, bless you as my
child, and all in my Universe treasure and love you fully this
and every day.*

*And so it is in my name, the Holy Mother-Father God
who created you and loves you unconditionally; the love,
light, and healing of the Christ; and the power of the Holy
Spirit that lives and moves in your being.*

Message from Spirit

Inner guidance sometimes appears when you find yourself making sudden and spontaneous decisions without knowing in advance the meaning behind them. To flow without question or hesitation with such decisions is the essence of living a guided life at the highest level. To fight or recant such sudden moments of Divine Guidance is to abandon your Spirit and derail from the highest flow in your life.

Morning Affirmation

I trust all spontaneous and organic decisions that leap from my deepest self as an indication and affirmation that my Divine Spirit is forever in charge of guiding my way. I am eager and willing to allow my Divine Spirit, in the way of spontaneous inner guidance, to surprise me and take over the direction of my life at any given moment. I delight in all sudden inner revelation springing forward from my most authentic Self, bypassing all premeditated thought or plan.

I trust implicitly and without question that each spontaneous response to life is a resounding *yes!* to my soul's holy plan and an indication that God is with me. I trust that the wisdom and value of such spontaneous revelations and shifts will be revealed in their own time, and I release my own timing as irrelevant. As a being eternally connected to all that is good for me in all ways, I do not need to understand why such impulses arise. I am patient and will wait for my Divine Spirit to make its great and intricate plan known to me in right time.

Today's Mantra

I am a spontaneous channel of light.

Your Personal Blessing

This is a joyful day, _____ (your name), as you are blessed with spontaneous wisdom and perfect divine intelligence.

Wisdom and truth will flow with ease in your every spoken word, every action, and every choice this day. You sparkle and shine with illumination, divine intelligence, instant revelation, and an unerring insight arising from a place beyond all ego or intellect. You have instant answers, absolute certainty, confidence, and perfect timing in all that unfolds from you and toward you.

I bless you with confidence and the faith to say yes to all the opportunities that unfold before you this day. I bless you to see beyond appearances, hear beyond words, sense beyond the physical, and understand beyond your intellect the truth in all things this day. You, _____ (your name), are the force of power and elegance behind all that moves into your path, as you command the moments unfolding before you to be in service to your Divine Spirit's bidding. Those with whom you speak will honor and respect your words, as they will feel the holy force of Divine wisdom pouring forth *from you. I bless you to flow easily and effortlessly toward your highest good without any hindrance from your ego or the world around throughout this day.*

And so it is in my name, the Holy Mother-Father God who created you and loves you unconditionally; the love, light, and healing of the Christ; and the power of the Holy Spirit that lives and moves in your being.

Message from Spirit

If you want to experience Divine Guidance operating in your life, as intended by the great Creator, it is necessary to respond to all subtle energetic vibrations coming to your attention with a resounding and embracing *yes!* When you affirm the value of all forms of inner guidance, it gains power in serving you.

Morning Affirmation

I trust life to work on my behalf at all times, and I therefore say a joyful and confident *yes!* to all experiences coming my way today. I feel the power of the Holy Spirit orchestrating all events that unfold before me this day to serve my highest good. I feel all heavenly forces of goodness quietly serving my Spirit behind the scenes, and I resist nothing positive that comes my way. I say yes to the absolute necessity and value of every condition and circumstance that occurs as I move through the day, and realize that nothing is accidental or incongruent with my soul's plan to merge with Spirit.

I fear nothing this day. I avoid nothing this day. I accept everything that unfolds as being in accordance with the divine plan of the Holy Spirit working through me and for my own benefit, even when the connection between my experience and the goodness hidden inside of it is not apparent to me. I fully surrender personal ego or negative judgment of all people or events that I encounter this day, and wholeheartedly accept that their presence is in service to my Spirit and my soul's learning and growth. I am confident that all that does not have purpose in my life and for my highest good will be removed before I encounter it, and I am grateful to say yes and receive the full goodness of whatever presents itself to me this day.

Today's Mantra

Yes!

Your Personal Blessing

I, your Holy Mother-Father God, Source of all life, and Creator of all things in the Universe, bless you, _____ (your name), with the highest order of love and support this day.

This day is a magical day, ordered by the great and living Creator, to serve you ceaselessly in achieving your highest potential. The angels will clear your path, and the joy guides will tickle your fancy. The helpers will open the way, and the teachers will provide the challenges you are ready to meet. Your healers will watch over your heart and keep your body healthy and safe. They are in service to your loving Creator's command to all in this realm and beyond to serve you as the heavenly child of the most high. Every person you encounter is a messenger of goodness for your soul and a light bearer of gifts.

Guidance

Every experience you have this day is orchestrated by God to lead you to more strength, more joy, more happiness, more abundance, and more peace of mind and body. As you walk through this day, you will be filled with wonder and surprise at the bounty of goodness flowing your way. And you will be humbled by the ceaseless love and tenderness of God directed toward you. Your day will be sprinkled with laughter, both from within and all around. The Universe sings in chorus with you a heavenly yes to all your heart desires.

And so it is in my name, the Holy Mother-Father God who created you and loves you unconditionally; the love, light, and healing of the Christ; and the power of the Holy Spirit that lives and moves in your being.

Message from Spirit

If you say yes when you mean no or no when you mean yes, you become disconnected from the flow of your Divine Inner Wisdom and get lost in the fearful and controlling confusion of the mind. Take the time you need to tune in to your true feeling, yes or no. Your feeling may even be, *I don't know . . . yet.* Pause before you speak, and be willing to wait for guidance to come. It will be felt if you are patient and allow time and breath for it to enter your heart. Be slow to speak before you feel guidance. Mean what you say and say what you mean. This is one of the greatest gifts of guidance you can offer yourself.

Morning Affirmation

I decide wisely and speak my truth with every word. I honor my right to personal boundaries and exercise this right in my honest and direct communication. I say yes, freely and with excitement, to that which I am open to, and I say no, without anxiety or fear, to those situations that do not support and honor my Spirit or respect my boundaries. I have the right to feel comfortable with my environment and to leave when my environment is not healthy and positive for me. I have a right to refrain from being involved in what is not my concern or personal business, and I can easily and quickly walk away from what no longer serves a positive purpose in my life or no longer respects and supports my Spirit.

I say yes to my Spirit and no to my old patterns and negative imprints from the past. I say yes to my authenticity and no to control over me by others. I say yes to needs and no to caretaking others who can take care of themselves. I say yes to inner light and no to my fearful thoughts. I take the time I need to feel my authentic Spirit speaking to me in my heart. I am free from others' coercion or influence to abandon my inner self. I am centered and empowered in my truth. I trust myself to speak my truth and do, without hesitation or fear.

Today's Mantra

I speak with a truthful yet loving heart.

Your Personal Blessing

Today, _____ (your name), I, your Holy Mother-Father God, who delights in your very existence, bless you with my unconditional love.

I bless your words as they fall from your lips, that they reflect and express the holy truth of your Divine Spirit. I bless you to create strong and healthy boundaries, leaving those around you who mean any harm or cause confusion, by simply walking the other way. I bless you, _____ (your name), this day with an aura of peace, and everywhere you go, a beautiful light will surround and emanate from your heart.

I bless you with the confidence to take your time and express your heart from a place of honesty and unwavering self-love. As you move through this day, all the people and circumstances you encounter will feel your beautiful Spirit, and respect and honor it deeply. I bless you with relaxation and ease, freeing you from all urgency and worry, and any overpowering energy of others. This day, I bless you with the ability to laugh easily, sing your heart song spontaneously, and express your needs freely and without confusion, knowing that those needs will be heard and respected with love toward you.

And so it is in my name, the Holy Mother-Father God who created you and loves you unconditionally; the love, light, and healing of the Christ; and the power of the Holy Spirit that lives and moves in your being.

Message from Spirit

Take your time and breathe deeply before you make decisions in your life. Look first for intuitive affirmation before you make commitments. Check the energy of every decision you make and wonder how it might affect your deepest self. Will this decision support your most authentic Self, or will it oppress it? Will it allow your true Spirit to shine, or hide it? Be courageous enough to sense what feels true for you in response to each possible choice, and then do that.

Morning Affirmation

I breathe deeply and check in with my inner guidance before I make any decision this day. I turn inward and feel the vibrational frequency that arises from my possible choices, and I look for resonance and truth in my heart as an indication that such a decision is good for my Spirit. I step away from the outside influences of others and lovingly check in with myself to examine whether a possible choice is in harmony and integrity with my heart before I decide. If I feel hesitation or a negative pull, discomfort, or resistance from my Spirit toward a particular choice, I will not make that choice.

I notice the difference between the response of my intellect and the feeling in my heart. While I will be open to consideration from my rational mind, I will allow my heart and inner guidance to make all final decisions this day. I trust that my inner guidance reflects more than is visible to my outer senses, and arises from beyond my intellect in present time. I sense what feels true for me and what feels out of harmony with my Spirit, and I am fearlessly courageous to trust my inner guidance and choose to follow it over everything else.

Today's Mantra

I trust my inner guidance even when it is difficult to understand.

Your Personal Blessing

Wake up and be happy, _____ (your name), as you move into this day. I, your Holy Mother-Father God, Creator of all life, bless you today with a keen sense of intuition that guides you each moment to your highest good.

Breathe deeply and easily as you comfortably tune inward to know your true direction. Your commitments will be made with clarity and confidence, and those with whom you enter into commitment will appreciate the blessing of their involvement with you. I bless you with a quiet and supportive mind, open to all your decisions, so that you follow your truth without question or interference. As you move through the day, I bless you with deep inner peace, which will be felt by those around you, and they, in turn, will open their hearts and minds and listen as you speak. Your guidance will serve not only your own soul's path to growth this day, but also those whom you touch with great clarity and insight.

I bless your projects and creative ideas so that they will be heard and supported by those with whom you work. I bless you with inspiration with each breath you take so that you find it very easy to say yes and no appropriately, moment to moment. I fill your aura with golden light, so that your heart will radiate with power and love for self and others, for all to feel and benefit from. This day I bless you to receive unwavering, energetically clear guidance from within, as the Holy Spirit moves through you and shows the way.

This day, _____ (your name), I bless you with the breath of life and fill you with peace and inner clarity. There is nothing to fear.

And so it is in my name, the Holy Mother-Father God who created you and loves you unconditionally; the love, light, and healing of the Christ; and the power of the Holy Spirit that lives and moves in your being.

Message from Spirit

Be strong and hold on to your authentic nature while navigating the whirlwinds of life. Do not allow yourself to be whisked away from your deepest needs and soulful longings by overbearing, aggressive people, or the useless opinions and intrusive persuasions offered by those who do not know or even care about your true self. Keep centered in your truth and trust your intuitive guidance always. It is the voice and force of your most authentic and Holy Spirit, your Divine Self. To do otherwise is to throw your life away.

Morning Affirmation

I am strong and unwavering in respecting and following my authentic Spirit no matter what is going on around me. I stay centered and grounded even in the company of aggressive and overwhelming people and influences. I turn my attention inward and seek the counsel and guidance of my Higher Self, and I refrain from soliciting the useless opinions of others to guide my way. I only seek input from those people whom I admire and who have undergone the very challenges I presently face and who have succeeded in achieving outcomes that I respect and admire.

Although I hear them, I do not internalize the random opinions of others, nor do I consider them evidence of my worth. I remain steadfast and true to my genuine Spirit even in the face of adversity and criticism. I am willing to withstand the disapproval of others over abandoning my Spirit, and I remain ever faithful to my true nature, my own values, and my integrity, even when I am challenged to give in. I allow only the power of Holy Spirit to move me through this day, and I invoke the one and same Holy Spirit to walk before me and banish all contrary influences on my path and in my thoughts and feelings. I am guided by the power of the Holy Spirit to remain true to myself with every step I take this and every day.

Today's Mantra

I am true to myself.

Your Personal Blessing

Today, _____ *(your name), I, your Holy Mother-Father God, Creator of Life, and Source of all things in the Universe, bless you with unwavering self-determination and absolute self-control in the face of all adversity and challenge.*

I bless you with the power to honor and express your true Spirit to its fullest this day. I bless you with the ability to effortlessly speak your truth, stand your ground, and remain faithful to your highest values, even in the face of opposition and assault. I proclaim that those who attempt to lead you astray or deter you from living your highest truth will stop in their tracks and cease their useless campaign. Instead they will surrender their negativity and turn to you for guidance and counsel. Others, even those in power, will respect and honor your Spirit, as they will feel the integrity and wholeness emanating in your vibration and aura.

I bless you with the ability to stand in the forces of darkness and shine your inner light bright and beautiful, instantly banishing all shadows and confusion, and raising the vibration surrounding you wherever you walk this day. I bless you with a calm, clear, and powerful vibration as you speak up and cease all disturbing or disrespectful influences that you encounter this day.

I bless you with the ability to easily walk away from all that is not in your highest good without a moment's hesitation. I bless you with the ability to withstand tension, challenge, drama, confrontation, or unrelenting outside persuasion without being distracted or falling into fear or doubt. I bless you, _____ (your name), with the ability to walk through the eye of any storm that unfolds this day without disturbance to, or deterrence from, living the truth of your Holy Spirit.

And so it is in my name, the Holy Mother-Father God who created you and loves you unconditionally; the love, light, and healing of the Christ; and the power of the Holy Spirit that lives and moves in your being.

Message from Spirit

Inner guidance is the activity of our personal "I" making contact with the greater Universal "I Am." It is the most undeniable affirmation that our Spirit is real and wants to move us through life. To follow inner guidance is to allow our Great Spirit, as opposed to our limited ego self, to navigate our personal journey through life. When we are following inner guidance without hesitation, we are in flow with our divine plan. To live without inner guidance is to live without a connection to our Source of life. This goes against our Divine makeup and is unnatural.

Morning Affirmation

I am in constant contact with my great "I Am" Divine and Holy Spirit this day. I accept all inner guidance as direct proof that my unconditionally loving Creator, my Holy Mother-Father God, is directly overseeing my life and in communication with me in every single thought I have, every feeling moving through my body, and every breath I take. My Spirit is guided by the light and power of the Divine Spirit throughout this day, and I am free of all negative or limiting imprints, mental or emotional patterns, bad habits, poor attitudes, and ingrained false perceptions carried over from my past experiences, this lifetime or before, and I live as a fully enlightened Spirit, fully present in this moment. I feel the love of the Holy Spirit for me in every single hunch, gut feeling, or intuitive insight that comes to my attention. I surrender my will to the will of my Creator and flow in the highest degree of living light this day.

Today's Mantra

The Holy Spirit is my guide.

Your Personal Blessing

Today, _____ (your name), I, Holy Mother-Father God, Creator of all life, bless you with gently felt guidance and clarity.

I bless your thoughts so that they are quiet and peaceful, and filled with love of self and love of your Creator. I bless your emotions so that they are light and carefree, and joyful in feeling the love the Universe has for you, now and always. I bless your physical body so that you feel healthy, strong, and flexible. I bless you with flexibility and agility of mind and body to respond to every subtle message and impulse that I, your Holy Mother-Father God who loves you unconditionally, send your way, without hesitation or resistance.

I bless you to trust your inner guidance and flow with it, having complete confidence in the outcome. I bless your Spirit to have dominion over your ego and soul, keeping them transfixed, listening and learning from the Divine Spirit within you. I bless your actions so that they flow in total harmony with your holy plan, and easily and quickly adjust whenever you drift away. I bless your work this day, that it may bring light and love to whomever it touches and affects. The angels and heavenly Spirit helpers in service to me, your Holy Mother-Father God, will make your way delightful. As you move through this day, you will walk free and unencumbered of any negative energy, as the helpers will stop and bind all that would interfere with the heavenly flow of God's light in your way.

And so it is in my name, the Holy Mother-Father God who created you and loves you unconditionally; the love, light, and healing of the Christ; and the power of the Holy Spirit that lives and moves in your being.

Message from Spirit

Once you embrace inner guidance, you begin to sense that the Universe is indeed brilliantly and perfectly organized to flow in absolute support of your soul's growth. You start to see how everything that occurs in your life is beautifully designed to assist you in reaching your fullest soul potential. Only by following the natural forces of your inner compass are you able to recognize that all is destined to ultimately go right for you. To implicitly trust inner guidance is to live in fearless faith and with deep and joyful confidence that your life is now and always a grand success.

Morning Affirmation

I accept that everything I experience this day flows in accordance with the divine plan, and is absolutely designed to support and assist my soul's highest growth in every way. Everything I encounter is beautifully orchestrated to help me achieve my heart's desire. Through my inner guidance, I recognize the behind-the-scenes assistance working on my behalf in all things and through all people. Nothing that I experience or encounter is out of order. Everything that comes my way this day is an important and essential component in achieving my goals and intentions for the day. I trust my inner guidance and follow my intuition as I feel it, and I know in my Spirit that everything is unfolding as it should.

The Universe is a loving and benevolent place, set up for my joyful life experience, and all experiences I enter into today are designed to perfectly unfold in service to my highest good and beyond my own personal expectations. I walk this day in fearless faith, knowing that the Universe is on my side and is set up for me to succeed in experiencing my heart's desires today.

Today's Mantra

The loving Universe is working for me.

Your Personal Blessing

Today, _____ (your name), I, the Holy Mother-Father God, who loves you unconditionally now and always, bless your Spirit with both obvious and hidden support in all that you do.

I bless your Spirit to say the perfect words at the perfect time in all conversations so that you are heard and understood with warm reception. I bless your Spirit to hear the deeper meaning behind all that other people share with you so that you are warm and receptive and understanding as well. I bless your Spirit with the perfection of arriving at every place you need to go with ease and flow, and at exactly the right moment for your pleasure and peaceful success. I bless your Spirit with unexpected support in the form of helpful and kind people who go out of their way to make your day pleasant. I bless your Spirit with surprising opportunities and openings that bring you abundance and comfort.

I bless your Spirit with people who watch your back, look out for you, and stand up for you in your absence. I bless your Spirit with good friends who want to help you succeed and who happily applaud and celebrate every success that you experience this day. I bless your Spirit with exciting invitations to enjoy life with loving others. I bless your Spirit with the opportunity to be a messenger of love and light to others so that your very presence is uplifting and healing to experience, and leaves those around you feeling grounded, calm, and peaceful.

I bless your Spirit with the power to change your mind when you feel it is appropriate and necessary without undue concern or overthinking. I bless your Spirit with the ability to convey your truth without diluting or hiding it in any way. I bless your Spirit to fill rooms with laughter and hearts with love. You, _____ (your name), walk in the invisible company of angels and Divine Spirit helpers who race ahead to clear your path and sweeten the way for your arrival. I bless your Spirit with charm, charisma, and beauty, bringing light and love to every situation you encounter this day.

And so it is in my name, the Holy Mother-Father God who created you and loves you unconditionally; the love, light, and healing of the Christ; and the power of the Holy Spirit that lives and moves in your being.

Message from Spirit

Inner guidance is the holy and powerful force inside us that wants us to be who we fully and most authentically are, not only the people we want to be but also who our Divine and loving Creator and the Source of all life has designed us to be. To follow our inner guidance is to connect our deepest inner force toward authenticity with the Universe's equal force and desire to connect with us. This energetic embrace is a great love affair between the individual "I" and the Divine "I Am."

Morning Affirmation

I am divinely guided this day to follow my intuition in all matters, as it leads me to express my most authentic Self. I allow my inner guidance to flow easily and comfortably into my conscious mind, where it then moves me in the direction in which my loving Creator wants me to move. I surrender all limiting personal intentions and open up to my Creator's highest intentions for me this day. I step out of my own way and make room in my mind and heart to express myself in a way that reflects my true Divine nature and overrides all negative imprints and limitations arising from my soul or ego.

As I move with my inner guidance toward my authentic heart's desire this day, I feel my Creator's love reaching out toward me and fully supporting and guiding my Spirit. As I flow with my Creator's great wisdom moving through me, I naturally spread the light of love and peace wherever I go and to whomever I touch. I feel the force of my loving Creator, the Holy Mother-Father God, embracing my heart through my intuition, and I relax into this holy embrace, filled with trust and gratitude that I am so deeply loved and guided by my Creator. I allow myself to discover new and hidden talents, and fearlessly explore them to their fullest. I leave behind the patterns of ego and soul that prevent me from living in accordance with my loving Creator's plan for me. I am fearlessly committed to being my greatest self and shining my brightest light this day.

Today's Mantra

Holy Spirit, move me to my fullest potential this day.

Your Personal Blessing

Today, _____ (your name), I, your ever-loving Holy Mother-Father God, Creator of the Universe, bless your Spirit with the warm embrace of my eternal, loving light.

I bless your Spirit to be filled with peace and inner serenity this day as your mind relaxes and moves in harmony with my loving guidance. I bless your heart to be wide open and receptive to feeling all holy subtle inner promptings reaching out to you. I bless your mind to recognize and embrace the force of the Holy Spirit flowing in you with each breath. I bless your Spirit to feel my love for you and allow your heart to overflow with love for yourself and all of life this day. I proclaim all irritation and impatience of ego and soul troubling your Spirit to give way to my patience and tolerance. I command all fear and agitation of ego and soul troubling your Spirit to give way to the confidence and peace of the Holy Spirit within.

I invoke inner music to flow through your sweet and powerful Spirit this day so that you will dance through your moments as though on a cloud. The sweet smell of fresh flowers from my heavenly garden will surround and engulf your aura, reassuring you with the loving companionship of the Nature Spirits, bringing their magical perfume to your senses and bathing your path with sweet surprises. I bless your Spirit, _____ (your name), so that you experience the fullness of heaven's glorious sun shining brightly in your heart, bringing warmth and joy to your inner being. Wherever your Spirit walks this day, the light and love of heaven will precede your footsteps and bring with you a lightness of heart. I bless you to gracefully and effortlessly move in tandem with the Holy Spirit, using it as your guide, your partner, your leader through every moment this day. I bless your Spirit with mental quiet so that you can hear heaven's love song to you.

And so it is in my name, the Holy Mother-Father God who created you and loves you unconditionally; the love, light, and healing of the Christ; and the power of the Holy Spirit that lives and moves in your being.

Message from Spirit

Without our natural inner guidance shedding light on our path, life feels like a dark and meaningless struggle. Without our inner light to brighten the path, all appears random and chaotic, even threatening and dangerous. It is only by becoming aware of the more subtle flow of energy that connects all of life, through our inner guidance, that we can sense the invisible connection, order, and deeper meaning behind all things. Without a clear sense of this connection between our personal selves and all things in life, it becomes nearly impossible to be genuinely creative and confidently authentic. Intuition is the bedrock of creativity. Inner guidance is the compass that leads our expression to one of great meaning and beauty.

Morning Affirmation

I follow the light of my inner guidance throughout this day, and refuse to allow any fearful ego thoughts, negative emotions, or surface appearances to scare me into believing that life is random, chaotic, or threatening to me in any way. I am safe, grounded, and fully protected this day, and I trust and move with the flow of my intuition moment by moment. I follow my inner guidance with ease and have no need to explain myself to others or question what I feel to be true. I sense and trust the hidden Divine order behind all unfolding events and circumstances in my life, and I accept that a higher divine plan is working on behalf of my personal good as well as that of all human beings on earth at all times.

I follow my inner guidance, knowing that it will lead me to new and creative opportunities to express my authentic Self and contribute to the greater good of all, in my own personal way, this day. I recognize and am extremely grateful for beauty all around me, and I use it today to inspire me to create even more beauty on the planet, through my words, actions, and deeds. I am a Divine co-creator with the Holy Mother-Father God, and my intuition is my magic compass, which leads me to golden opportunities this and every day.

Today's Mantra

Intuition is my path to creativity.

Your Personal Blessing

Today, _____ (your name), I, your ever-loving Holy Mother-Father God, Creator of the Universe, bless your Spirit to quickly rise above all negative energy and be immune to all fear-based negative thoughts coming your way, whether from within or from others.

I bless you to move in harmony with intuition in peaceful confidence and to be free of all need to defend or explain this choice to anyone. I bless you with a deep awareness of the hidden connection between you and all good things in life, and to flow with such goodness without pause or interruption. I bless you to be enlightened with empowering creative ideas and inspirations throughout this day, and to be showered with beauty and appreciation in every direction you walk and from every person you meet.

I bless you _____ (your name), to be guided by the pulse of heavens and flow with the perfect divine plan that moves you toward your highest creative success this day. I bless you with the insight to see past appearances and recognize opportunity present in every person you meet at every turn. I bless you with the support and applause of your family to trust you and respect your intuition without question or doubt. I bless you to receive abundant financial and emotional support to meet your needs flawlessly, and with more to spare and share. I bless you to be the bearer of light wherever you go and to inspire those around with new and creative ideas to replace frustration and despair.

And so it is in my name, the Holy Mother-Father God who created you and loves you unconditionally; the love, light, and healing of the Christ; and the power of the Holy Spirit that lives and moves in your being.

Message from Spirit

Our becoming disconnected from the force of inner guidance is the root of all violence, whether toward others or ourselves. With inner guidance in place, we feel safe, calm, and grounded. We also cannot ignore that every thought, every choice, every act emanating from us affects both us and others. Inner guidance is the source of wisdom that leads to peace, both within and without. Without inner guidance, peace is not possible.

Morning Affirmation

I am peaceful and calm this day, knowing that I am fully provided for in every way. I fear no one and nothing as I am guided to be in the flow of my highest creative and intuitive consciousness, manifesting all that is necessary to fulfill my needs, and to provide support and abundance to others. I bring peace with me wherever I go, and calm the fires of agitation and aggression in the hearts and minds of the people who surround me. I ease tension and open hearts with my vibration, and release fear of lack in others, causing them to let go of competition and attack as a means of feeling safe and secure. I welcome my role as a provider and source of comfort and peace to the world.

I walk in patience and tolerance for differences I encounter with others, and seek to learn from others and grow in my understanding of those with whom I must engage on a deeper level. I recognize the Holy Spirit in all people, and live with great respect and appreciation for the many ways in which God manifests through us. I am an agent of peace and a healer of violence. I forgive all who have violated my inner peace, and I ask forgiveness from all whose peace I have disturbed. I walk though this day with serenity and acceptance of all that comes my way.

Today's Mantra

I am peaceful and safe.

Your Personal Blessing

Today, _____ (your name), I, your ever-loving Holy Mother-Father God, Creator of the Universe, bless your Spirit to walk in peace and be the bearer of peace wherever you go and to all whom you touch.

I bless you to be filled with a deep love of self and others as you recognize the Holy Spirit dwelling in all. I bless your Spirit with infinite patience and deep understanding and compassion for all people, and especially for those who are particularly challenging and difficult to work with this day. I bless your Spirit with the ability to turn confrontations into compromises and to help people let go of their rigid mental stances and positions, and enter into a more receptive and open capacity to listen and learn new perspectives and ways of thinking.

Guidance

I bless your Spirit, _____ (your name), to radiate with pure tranquility and personal freedom. I bless your Spirit with inner silence and the acute ability to hear not only the words but also the meaning behind the words coming to you this day. I bless your Spirit with loving effervescence and childlike joy as you express your ideas and creative plans. I bless your Spirit to fully enjoy life and bring enjoyment to others in their interaction with you.

And so it is in my name, the Holy Mother-Father God who created you and loves you unconditionally; the love, light, and healing of the Christ; and the power of the Holy Spirit that lives and moves in your being.

Message from Spirit

Every impulse arising from our internal guidance has meaning. The challenge is to discover what that meaning is. It is not possible to figure out, through intellectual means alone, the meaning arising from the Spirit. We must surrender our intellect over to the heart, and let it inform us of the meaning of all that we energetically sense and feel. We can, however, borrow the power of personal expression to assist in our quest for understanding.

Morning Affirmation

I recognize that every impulse, *aha* moment, gut feeling, or intuition that comes to my awareness has meaning and importance for me this day. I am open to all messages that I receive from Spirit as personalized guidance sent in order for me to arrive at my heart's desire in a safe and grounded way, free of interruption or distraction, and without wandering toward the wrong course of thinking or action. I direct my subconscious mind to intercept all intuitive sensations, thoughts, feelings, or inner knowing, and interpret them correctly and in timely fashion in order to help me stay the course toward my highest good and in service to my Divine Creator this day.

I instruct my intellect to pay close attention to all that I hear, see, touch, taste, and smell, not missing a single important detail that can serve to best inform me as I move along my creative path this day. I turn each detail over to my heart for accurate interpretation and understanding. I trust my heart to guide my intellect when it comes to making my decisions this day, as I know that my heart conveys the path of my most authentic and Divine Spirit to my conscious mind now and every day.

Today's Mantra

I listen to my heart.

Your Personal Blessing

Today, _____ (your name), I, your ever-loving Holy Mother-Father God, Creator of the Universe, bless your Spirit to move with the powerful and divinely inspired flow of your intuition, recognizing it as a heart song sent to you from the heavens to chart your course and guide your way to all that is most beautiful, all loving, most constructive for your personal goals, and in service to my holy plan for you.

I bless you to see the truth, sense the truth, feel the truth, and touch the truth lying in the subtle vibration of all that appears on your path. I bless your thinking mind to observe and report to your heart and your Divine Spirit therein all that you experience, and to surrender fully and with clarity and confident obedience to all that your heart guides you toward this day. I bless your path to open up and flow directly toward your highest and most successful outcomes, leading

*you without diversion to our most beautiful gifts and bless-
ings in store for you this day.*

*I bless your Spirit, _____ (your name),
this day to be a leader to others, encouraging them, by example, to trust and follow their hearts, bringing all into peaceful
collaboration and creative invention of the highest order. I
bless your Spirit to speak loudly and clearly to you this day,
through your physical five senses and through a keen sensitivity to all subtle vibrations emanating toward you from all
directions, keeping you attuned to all levels of activity surrounding and affecting you this day.*

*I bless your heart, dear one, to know, without thinking,
pausing, or hesitating, the best course to follow, the best decisions to make, and the best, most accurate means of understanding all people and events that unfold before you this day.
I bless the light of the Holy Spirit to shine within you, around
you, toward you, and with each step you take, brightening the
way for others to trust and follow your guidance without fear
or struggle, giving way to profound insight and peace flowing
from you in all directions and toward all people.*

*And so it is in my name, the Holy Mother-Father God
who created you and loves you unconditionally; the love,
light, and healing of the Christ; and the power of the Holy
Spirit that lives and moves in your being.*

Message from Spirit

Voice what you feel arising from the heart space and pay attention to the vibration it carries. If what you voice resonates with your inner guidance, you will feel its truth in your bones. There will be no question as to whether or not it is "right." It will feel true. Therefore, do not keep your intuitive feelings bottled up. Express them out loud and often—not for the approval of others, but for your own personal energetic examination. What you name, you claim. In other words, the more you voice your intuition, the more value you place on it. The more you value inner guidance, the stronger, clearer, and more influential it becomes in your life.

Morning Affirmation

I speak with clarity and from the heart this day, and I listen for the truth resonating in my own words as I speak. I speak my heart's truth openly and freely, without interruption, argument, or distraction from my intellect. I am free of the fear of others' opinions, and I stand powerfully in the truth of my Spirit, even when others challenge or seek to discredit me. I respectfully listen to others but do not allow anyone to sway me from honoring and expressing my intuition and living fully by its wisdom. I closely examine the vibration of my own spoken and inner words this day, searching for the affirmation of truth in their vibration.

I do not hesitate to change my direction if, for any reason, I do not feel the vibration of truth coming from that which I consider and speak. My body serves to mirror the truth quickly and accurately back to me by the vibrations I experience, serving as a reliable compass to chart my way. When I suspect something is out of integrity with the flow to my highest good, I will speak it out loud and test its vibration by the sound of my own words. If the words I speak are in harmony with my Spirit, I will sense it in the vibration they send out. If the vibration is harmonious, I will trust and follow these ideas as true guidance and intuition. If I do not feel resonance and confirmation of truth in my heart as I speak, I will ignore and leave such ideas behind.

When I am listening to others, I listen from the heart for the vibration and resonance of truth, as it pertains to my path in that moment. If the vibration resonates with truth and my heart feels the light, I will engage in peace. If I sense a lack of resonance or truth, I will peacefully disengage and walk away, without fear or worry of condemnation. My ears serve as watchful guardians to protect me and keep me on course, listening for truth and warning me away from deception, either from others or from my own negative thought patterns and beliefs. I speak my truth and listen for truth in all I hear.

Today's Mantra

I listen for truth.

Your Personal Blessing

Today, _____ *(your name), I, your ever-loving Holy Mother-Father God, Creator of the Universe, bless your Spirit to sense the truth behind all ideas, considerations, events, and actions as you move peacefully through this day.*

I bless your Spirit with a keen and unerring ability to distinguish the vibration of truth from that of error, false perception, or misleading thoughts, beliefs, or information. I bless you with the power of Spirit to withstand all criticism and condemnation from others, with an unwavering faithfulness to your truth and a forgiving but unmoved heart to stay faithful to your true intuition and guidance. I bless you with the protection of a thousand guardian angels to remain steadfast and fearless in trusting your inner wisdom this day, and I send the forces of light and wisdom to enlighten the minds and hearts of those who challenge or condemn you so that they stop interfering with the flow of your authentic Self.

I bless your Spirit to speak from the heart, with loving and brave words that flow from your intuition as guided by the Holy Spirit in you. I bless your Spirit, _____ (your name), to ignore all criticism, dispersions, and assault on your authentic Self, rendering all such efforts powerless and impotent, without the ability to affect you. I bless your Spirit to speak freely and to change course immediately and without pause when you drift away from truth.

I bless your Spirit to empower others to speak their authentic truth in your presence and to allow you to listen to their words as they speak, choosing only those words that serve the highest good, and loving blessings and intentions for all. I bless your Spirit to speak with clarity, insight, understanding, and love for self and others, in all company and with all people, no matter their status or position in your life.

I bless your Spirit to receive the love and respect of all people, that they may sense your good and authentic heart, your loving intentions, and your courageous Spirit to stand by your truth, giving you their full attention and utmost appreciation.

And so it is in my name, the Holy Mother-Father God who created you and loves you unconditionally; the love, light, and healing of the Christ; and the power of the Holy Spirit that lives and moves in your being.

Message from Spirit

Inner guidance cannot be felt if our hearts are closed, defended, or barricaded against life. To receive inner guidance, we must have the courage to feel all of our feelings. Even painful feelings enlighten. When the heart is blocked and feeling is ignored, the inner light is snuffed out and darkness descends all around. Feelings are the messengers of inner guidance. Let them flow and get the message. Once the message is received, the feeling subsides.

Morning Affirmation

I open my heart this day, fully and without fear, to feel the full depth of all my feelings and intuitions. My feelings are important intuitive messengers, and I embrace and respect all of them to serve as loving guidance for my soul. I am willing to feel the discomfort and even pain that may come with some of my feelings, knowing that even in this form, they are nevertheless necessary for my soul to experience and learn from as my soul grows to merge with my Spirit. I release all blockages of my heart that occurred in my less-informed past, forgiving all those who did not respect or treat me as I wanted and deserved to be treated.

I release blocked feelings from the past, and choose to be free, no longer governed by old fears and frozen in past experiences that are locked in my heart. I open my heart space and release everything from the past, this lifetime and all previous lifetimes, giving myself over to allow the full range of feelings and the messages they carry, and then fully and freely release all these past emotions and feelings into the loving care of the Holy Spirit who watches over me.

I am not afraid to experience and express my feelings in a healthy and loving way. I understand that they are the foundation upon which my inner guidance can provide my direction. I forgive myself for carrying feelings toward others and myself that do not serve my highest good, and I release them now. I forgive and release people who have hurt me in the past, and I accept the purpose they played in teaching me lessons that served my soul's growth. I listen to my feelings and allow them to come and then move on, having received the message. I open my heart this day and fully share it with others.

Today's Mantra

I open my heart.

Your Personal Blessing

Today, _____ (your name), I, your ever-loving Holy Mother-Father God, Creator of the Universe, bless your Spirit to walk with an open and fully receptive heart, feeling and expressing all of your emotions in a healthy and loving way.

I bless your Spirit to be free of the past and to be fully present in this moment, able to access and receive all intuitive guidance arising within your heart moment by moment this day, with peaceful understanding and nonattached love. I bless your Spirit to fully love all the people in your life, free of bias, insecurity, attachment, manipulation, and control. I bless your Spirit to be free and protected from the unconscious attachments and fears of others, and unencumbered by their clumsy attempts to attach or control you. I bless your Spirit to be immune to the negative effects of others' emotional anxiety cast into the atmosphere so that you are peaceful and grounded in the certainty that everything unfolds in divine order and all is well. I bless your Spirit to be immune to the emotional dramas of power and control of others, as you freely and fearlessly love yourself and accept yourself as a Divine Being. I bless you to be free of the need for others' approval to feel safe and secure.

I bless your Spirit, _____ (your name), to pull back the veil of illusion this day and recognize all your emotions as mediums for intuitive direction, receiving them fully, learning from them quickly, and releasing them from your heart space so that you walk without defense or unnecessary protection. I bless your Spirit to be free of all emotions that have no purpose or do not serve your soul's growth. I bless your Spirit to be filled with gladness and joy this day, knowing in your heart that I, your Holy Mother-Father God, take great pleasure in your existence, and celebrate and delight in your every experience this day as you find your way back to me, back to Source, love and light of the Universe.

And so it is in my name, the Holy Mother-Father God who created you and loves you unconditionally; the love, light, and healing of the Christ; and the power of the Holy Spirit that lives and moves in your being.

Message from Spirit

The first organ to be developed in the body is the human heart. It beats long before the brain is ever formed. It is the heart, not the brain, that guides the development of the embryo to create the full human vessel of the body. It has been your guidance system from the very beginning. Let it lead as it is naturally designed to.

Morning Affirmation

Today I lead from my heart, as I recognize it to be the first and most important source of intelligence with which to lead my life. My heart is a conscious center of awareness, and I trust it to guide me in every way. I listen to my heart over the thoughts and opinions of others, and over all outside sources of influence. I pay attention to all I learn today and turn it over to my heart for final affirmation of my best course in this day. My soul and ego are students of my heart. They follow its guidance and willingly trust the direction my heart points to, letting go of all defensive, judgmental perceptions of myself and others, and replacing these limiting and pain-inducing perceptions with love.

My heart guides me to my authentic Spirit and assists me in letting go of my past definitions of who I am, allowing me to freely and fully live as the holy light being that I truly am. My heart is in direct communication with the most loving forces of the Universe, who assist me in every way to co-create a more loving personal experience on earth, and spread more love and peace to those around me. I am not afraid, for my heart guides me to live, learn, and let go of all human ego attachments and live in Spirit. My soul is enlightened by the wisdom pouring through my heart, coming from the Holy Spirit that guides me. I am in perfect harmony with life as I flow from the Spirit in my heart.

Today's Mantra

My heart leads.

Your Personal Blessing

Today, _____ (your name), I, your everloving Holy Mother-Father God, Creator of the Universe, bless your Spirit to be guided by the Holy Spirit flowing from your heart, so that you live and move through time and space as an enlightened being.

I bless your Spirit to be in command of all situations that you face today, listening deep within for guidance before you speak or act. I bless your Spirit to fill your physical body, especially the heart, with unlimited divine energy and prefect vitality. I bless your Spirit to release those around you from their emotional pain and the agony of their negative thoughts, and help them find peace in their hearts as they experience your presence. I bless you to bring calm and confidence with you in all situations that you enter. Your friends and family *will relax and become stronger as you lead them back to their own inner wisdom and Divine Guidance by your example.*

Your loving vibration of clear insight and certainty of direction will touch the lives of those who are off course, and return them to their true path of authentic living. I bless your Spirit, _____ (your name), to be recognized this day as a true healer and teacher to others, by your easy manner, your loving vibration, and the Holy light of Spirit in your eyes. I bless your Spirit this day to know who you are, my Divine and treasured child, a holy and empowered co-creator with me in the Universe, and to live in accordance with your birthright to create miracles and free yourself from all bondage of ego and soul, now and forever.

And so it is in my name, the Holy Mother-Father God who created you and loves you unconditionally; the love, light, and healing of the Christ; and the power of the Holy Spirit that lives and moves in your being.

Message from Spirit

Inner guidance reveals to us that the Universe is in fact a friendly and loving place, and that all the events and people we encounter in life want to assist us in achieving our highest soul expression. Intuition is the guiding force that assures us on the deepest level that we can fully expect to receive all that we need in life in order to succeed. It is this same force that reminds us that what we do receive is something that our souls need in order to fulfill their highest growth potential. This Divine guiding force shows us that in the end, on a soul level, all in life is good and well.

Morning Affirmation

I am open and receptive to all the loving support the Universe has in store for me this day. I suspend all my previously held false and limiting ego and soul perceptions, and recognize that the way things naturally unfold today is for my highest good. I fully accept that I am a Holy Spirit embodied in human form, here to grow my soul. I embrace all that occurs as necessary to merge my human consciousness with my Holy Spirit and Source, my Creator. No matter what unfolds this day, I recognize that it is in accordance with my soul plan for growth at the highest level, and I gratefully and fully embrace all experiences that come my way, knowing that they are there to help me.

I feel the support and wisdom of the Universe unfolding before me with every experience, and I am humble in knowing that God's plan for me is filled with far more love, generosity, and blessings than any plan I could ever devise for myself. I expect success in every area of my life today, as I am a student who is open and willing to learn all that I can to elevate my soul and connect with my Spirit. I recognize and accept every person I meet as an ally in my soul plan, and I acknowledge the Holy Spirit in each and every situation unfolding before me. I am grateful for the intricate and perfect support in all things coming my way, and I gratefully accept the love and blessings the Universe has for me now and always.

Today's Mantra

I trust God's divine order, which is working for me this day.

Your Personal Blessing

Today, _____ (your name), I, your ever-loving Holy Mother-Father God, Creator of the Universe, bless your Spirit to experience the most supportive, positive, and loving encounters for your soul's growth.

I bless your Spirit to engage with people who respect and love your Spirit, and to fully understand and embrace your highest intentions. I bless your Spirit to fearlessly commit your full heart and soul to accept and embrace all challenges set before you this day as evidence of your growth, and to meet them with confidence and purity of Spirit, knowing that you will succeed. I bless your Spirit, _____ (your name), to laugh out loud at your fear, your weaknesses, your defenses, and to ask, often and without hesitation, for help from those around you, knowing that each one has been positioned by me, your loving Holy Mother-Father God, to stand by your side and lovingly guide you to the most positive and joyful outcome.

I bless you to learn new and empowering lessons this day, and to be especially open to ideas and concepts that invite you to live more fully and authentically as yourself, knowing there is no higher or more loving way to bless the world and the people in it. I bless your Spirit to overlook all irritating or obnoxious behaviors of others, and to find in your experience of them an opportunity to love more, forgive more, and relax more fully in your Holy Spirit. I bless you to step into your highest degree of personal loving power and engage in the events of the day with integrity, confidence, and a willingness to ask for help without fear, and be open to receiving love and support as your divine birthright as my holy child.

And so it is in my name, the Holy Mother-Father God who created you and loves you unconditionally; the love, light, and healing of the Christ; and the power of the Holy Spirit that lives and moves in your being.

Message from Spirit

Inner guidance reveals in increments the grand Spiritual blueprint we must follow to build a beautiful and meaningful life. When we embrace inner guidance to its fullest, we also fully embrace all that occurs to us with great love and deep acceptance and appreciation as part of our great Divine soul plan.

Morning Affirmation

I welcome all that I experience this day as an integral part of my soul's divine plan to merge with my Holy Spirit and be at one with my Source and Creator, Holy Mother-Father God of all creation. I listen with a deep inner awareness to my intuition and follow its promptings in full confidence that it leads to all that is necessary and valuable to grow my soul. I surrender my mind and body to the influence and guidance of my inner teacher, and flow with the subtle hints that point me in the direction of my greatest good and most profound opportunities throughout this day.

My heart is open, and I am clear and receptive to the deeper meaning behind all things that I encounter. I look past appearance for the true messages sent my way. I am aware of the many angels and guides constantly overseeing my path and placing gifts and blessings directly in front of me. I ask to be of service this day and for the Holy Spirit to use me in every instance where I can bring relief to another's suffering, ease to another's stress, and calm to another's anxiety. I offer myself as a messenger of love and blessings to all those around me and see every moment as one designed by the Holy Mother-Father uniquely for me to discover and express my own divine and loving nature. I accept all with an open and wise heart, and take nothing personally, no matter how irritating or upsetting to my human ego it may be. Instead I laugh, seeing the humor behind all events, and recognize God's subtle plan at work for me.

Today's Mantra

All that unfolds ultimately works in my favor.

Your Personal Blessing

Today, _____ (your name), I, your ever-loving Holy Mother-Father God, Creator of the Universe, bless your Spirit to be of service to humanity.

I bless your Spirit to act as healer to those whose hearts are heavy, while preventing any heaviness of heart from others to befall you. I bless your Spirit to bring relief to others' stress and anxiety, by calming and quieting their nervous systems, and elevating others' personal vibration to one of peace and relaxation with your kind words. I bless your Spirit to delight those in darkness on your path this day with your lightness of heart, your humor, and your playfulness. I bless your Spirit to restore balance and harmony to those who are in fear.

I bless your Spirit, _____ (your name), to walk as an ambassador of love on the planet today, reminding others, by your sensitive and caring words and actions, of the need to be patient and kind with one another and with yourself. I bless your Spirit to be graceful under pressure and able to maximize your time so that you have all the time you need this day to accomplish all your tasks and goals without tension or urgency. I bless your Spirit with free time to breathe, relax, and enjoy this beautiful day and take in all gifts and blessings that it has to share with you. I bless your Spirit to release the tensions and fears of your past, and to live fully and freely in peace in this moment.

The angels and guides will direct you to your greatest opportunities to be of service to our holy Creator, and give you the courage and confidence to embrace such moments fully without hesitation or resistance. I bless your Spirit to be a divine inspiration to those who have lost touch with their inner light, and to reconnect them to their holy and loving Source, simply by being in your presence. I bless your Spirit to take charge this day and lead from beginning to end in harmony, and flow with your soul's divine plan for growth, with absolute knowledge that all unfolds does so to serve you.

And so it is in my name, the Holy Mother-Father God who created you and loves you unconditionally; the love, light, and healing of the Christ; and the power of the Holy Spirit that lives and moves in your being.

Message from Spirit

If you desire to activate or strengthen the Divine force of inner guidance in your life, simply open your heart and let love be your motivating factor. If this is the force that consciously motivates you day by day, inner guidance will naturally move you.

Morning Affirmation

I activate the divine force of intuition coming to me from my Higher Self, the voice of the Holy Spirit within me, to move me this day. I open my heart fully to receive all loving impulses from my Higher Self, and I direct my subconscious mind to accept and respond to these impulses and directions immediately, without interruption or interpretation by my logical mind.

Holy Spirit, please remove all obstacles to my intuition, whether they are in the form of willful mental patterns, past imprints, the interfering opinions of others, telepathic influences, personal fear, others' fear, or unknown influences, allowing only you to guide me through this day. I consciously flow in the light and power of the Holy Mother-Father God and Holy Spirit this day and readily ignore all other influences and forces, known or unknown, coming my way. I am moved by love. I speak with love. I make decisions based only on love. I love my Spirit this day, and I give the Holy Spirit full control to create this day with love.

Today's Mantra

I intuitively flow with love.

Your Personal Blessing

Today, _____ (your name), I, your ever-loving Holy Mother-Father God, Creator of the Universe, bless your Spirit to clearly and consciously receive all guidance and direction coming from me to you, and to ignore all else.

I bless your Spirit to be filled with love for your holy self—body, mind, and emotions—and to share this love with all living beings. I bless and protect your Spirit from all negative energy, known and unknown, on all vibrational levels and in all forms. I bless your Spirit to be free of all attempts from others of mental or emotional bondage and control over you, and I endow you with the strength of the Holy Spirit to walk in absolute peace and clarity this day. I bless your Spirit to intuitively follow your highest path this day, and to deeply and accurately sense the needs and wishes of others you encounter and make clear, conscious decisions on how to best and most lovingly respond to those needs while remaining loving and respectful to yourself. I bless your Spirit with the power, the light, the support, and the assistance of the heavens to remove all obstacles and blind spots this day so that you clearly feel and sense the force of intuition directing your path away from danger and diversion, and keeping you on the road to higher and higher divine expression.

I bless your Spirit to speak only with love, silencing all other words and thoughts that would attempt to diminish your power and light. I bless your Spirit, _____
(your name), to completely avoid or quickly walk away from people or situations that are not in harmony with your divine purpose. I bless your Spirit to bring a peaceful, loving light to the hearts of your family, your neighbors, your friends, and your enemies so that all illusion of separation dissolves, and cooperation and peace between you and all others take its place. I bless your Spirit to take great pleasure and enjoyment in the manifestation of your creative heart's desire this day, so that you succeed beyond your wildest dreams and expectations, as a direct result of following your inner guidance and all light and love sent to you by the Holy Spirit through the voice of your Higher Self.

And so it is in my name, the Holy Mother-Father God who created you and loves you unconditionally; the love, light, and healing of the Christ; and the power of the Holy Spirit that lives and moves in your being.

Message from Spirit

We are not outside of Spirit looking in, mental window-shoppers wishing for enlightenment, but rather a spark of light inside Spirit, an essential part of the one great Universe. To know this from the deepest part of our being is the greatest guidance we can experience. There is no "out there" to run from, get to, or strive for. There is only internal awareness of what is true of our own nature to discover. Let this be the guidance we seek.

Morning Affirmation

I am completely surrounded and enveloped by the divine light of the Holy Spirit and the eternal love of the Holy Mother-Father God with each step I take throughout this day. I am never outside the holy light of God, my loving Creator and Source, who provides for all my needs. Each moment of this day, I am guided by the Holy Spirit, who shines divine light brightly upon my path. By this light I am made aware of the perfect action to take in every situation I meet, and I am automatically and gracefully moved in the best direction for my highest good at all times. I feel secure and confident in my actions and efforts, knowing that I am being guided by the love and light of the Holy Spirit as I work and play.

I am prepared for this day, facing all that I encounter with a cheerful smile, a peaceful and loving heart, and a calm and grounded response. I trust what I feel and know to be true in my heart, and I respect and follow my authentic feelings and intuition in every situation and with every person I meet, knowing that my choices reflect the divine light of my Spirit at all times. I am grateful for the loving embrace and unceasing light of my Creator's protection all around me this day. I am strong and capable, relaxed, and at ease in my Creator's care.

Today's Mantra

I walk in the light and love of God.

Your Personal Blessing

Today, _____ (your name), I, your ever-loving Holy Mother-Father God, Creator of the Universe, bless your Spirit and encase you in my never-ending light of guidance.

I bless your Spirit to enter into all commitments with unwavering confidence and unbridled enthusiasm, and I inspire you with intelligence, creativity, and wisdom in every challenge that you face. I bless your Spirit to gain the support and cooperation of others in all projects, conversations, and interactions, and I endow you with the power to distance and disconnect quickly, and steal away from those who seek to create drama, discord, and conflict as a means of gaining attention or deflecting from their own responsibilities. I bless your Spirit to speak with dignity and authority, quieting all internal discord, as well as discord with others.

I bless your Spirit to shine with the light of the Holy Spirit as you go about your business this day, leaving others inspired and uplifted as you touch their hearts. I bless your Spirit, _____ (your name), so that you feel cheerful and optimistic this day, taking great satisfaction in your efforts and knowing that you are being divinely guided by me, through the Holy Spirit, as you work. I bless your Spirit to be relaxed so that you enjoy the moments unfolding before you this day, rejuvenated by fresh food and drink, and nurtured by the companionship of delightful, loving friends and family. I bless you to experience spontaneous laughter and warm affection from those around you, recognizing the Spiritual kinship you share with all beings.

I bless your Spirit to be in command of this day, leading with your intuition and supporting all your decisions with swift and sound, confident action. I bless your Spirit with quiet moments of meditation and prayer this day, free of stress or urgency to take you away from time with me, your loving Holy Mother-Father God, Source of all life. I bless you to feel my light and presence in your heart and see it radiate all around you, touching everyone you meet, and filling their hearts and minds with light and love as quickly as their next breath. I bless your Spirit to be filled with the heavenly songs of my angels and your Spirit companions, their music dancing upon your ears. I bless your Spirit to be gifted with sweet-scented flowers from my earthly gardens, and your environment to be beautified with sun rays dancing all around.

And so it is in my name, the Holy Mother-Father God who created you and loves you unconditionally; the love, light, and healing of the Christ; and the power of the Holy Spirit that lives and moves in your being.

GIFTS

Message from Spirit

Breath is life. Breath is Spirit. Breath is the force of the Mighty "I Am" Holy Spirit pulsing through your being at this moment. Without breath there is no life. Your Divine Creator bestows upon you the breath of life. Allow the gift of breath, of life, to course through your being. Accept the holy force through the breath flowing into you. Do not resist or hold your breath, thus refusing the Holy Spirit entrance. Breathe the gift of life into your entire being.

Invocation

Most Holy Mother-Father God, through the power in you, I invoke the gift of breath to flow ever more deeply through my being, cleansing and releasing from my mind, body, and nervous system all that has passed, leaving me free and clear to live fully and unencumbered in the present moment. I call upon the power of the Holy Spirit, the breath of life within me, to fill me with vibrant life force and energy, so that I may live as an empowered and creative being this day. Let the gift of breath flow through me, bringing clear awareness of Spirit in all things to influence my every response and choice today. Allow me to more fully embrace this most precious gift of life, and to breathe in deeply before I speak and act today. Through my breath, allow the Holy Spirit to flow freely through me, to enlighten and inform my choices and guide my way.

Today's Mantra

I am gifted with the holy breath of life, and I am empowered.

Your Personal Blessing

Today, _____ (your name), I, your ever-loving Holy Mother-Father God, Creator of the Universe, bless your most glorious Spirit with the gift of the Holy Spirit coursing through your entire being.

I bless you with the gift of life, and I celebrate your being. As you walk this day, you will radiate with the goodness and sweetness that I have breathed into your body and brought forward with your birth. I bless you with a radiant and peaceful Spirit, _____ (your name), so that you know that you are deeply loved and treasured by heaven and by your Holy Mother-Father God, who called you forward into life. I bless you with freedom from all negative and disdainful projections, making you immune to all confused distortions that would convince you to dare consider yourself less than the most beloved creative being on earth that I have created you to be and that you are.

I bless you with a deep and unmovable connection to me, your holy Source for all in life, so that you are free to express your delightful authentic nature without hesitation or fear. I bless you to shine the light of Spirit wherever you go, being noticed and appreciated by all for your brilliant eyes *and glorious smile. I bless you with breath of life, the greatest of all gifts, to enjoy and create this earthly journey with the freedom to do as you choose, and to learn to become the master of your human experience. I bless you with the support of my heavenly angels, nature devas, joy guides, and divine helpers, so that your path is cleared as you journey this day and all days. I bless you to have a day sprinkled with laughter, in which you are light of heart, grounded in Spirit, and filled with the breath of life.*

And so it is in my name, the Holy Mother-Father God who created you and loves you unconditionally; the love, light, and healing of the Christ; and the power of the Holy Spirit that lives and moves in your being.

Message from Spirit

Open your heart and allow the gift of generosity to flow through you. Cheerfully share all that you possess with those in genuine need, without desire for return, knowing in confidence that all that is given in love will be replenished a thousandfold. Be a messenger of Source, relieving the pain and anxiety in others whenever possible through sharing your Spirit, your wealth, your resources, for all that you have has been given to you as well, as a gift from the great Creator. The more you freely use the gift of generosity already present in your heart, the more enriched your own life will become.

Invocation

Most Holy Mother-Father God, Creator, and Source of all life, by the power you bestow upon me, I call upon the gift of generosity to flow through my being this day, to enhance everything and everyone in my path. I invoke the angels of giving to move through me this day and allow me to share my heart with eagerness and joy, giving genuine support to those who are in need. I call forward words of gratitude and acknowledgment to generously flow from my lips to the people I am blessed to connect with today. Let my heart freely express love and appreciation toward all people I meet. I call upon the angels and guides of benevolence to work through me to help others, so that I reach out, lend a hand, offer a kind word or assistance without the need for personal recognition. By the power of the Spirit in me, I liberally share the goodness in me with the world today.

Today's Mantra

I am gifted with generosity, and I am empowered.

Your Personal Blessing

Today, _____ (your name), I, your ever-loving Holy Mother-Father God, Creator of the Universe, bless your Spirit with the gift of generosity, empowering you to freely share your love and light, wealth, goodness, and talent with all who cross your path.

I bless you with the companionship and support of the great heavenly Spirit helper, Saint Nicholas, who exemplifies and shares with you and through you endless abundance, replenishing what you share in Spirit, tenfold, a hundredfold, a thousandfold, and more, so that as you give, you receive back from me so quickly that you cannot possibly contain all of your blessings. I bless you with many surprising opportunities this day to remind your fellow human travelers of the abundance that is also theirs to enjoy, by your acts of generosity and sharing in my name. I decree that your every act is a blessing to others.

I bless you again and again, _____ (your name), with unimagined treasures from my heavenly kingdom, rewarding you for your generous and bountiful nature, bringing all that is dormant in and around you back to life, all that is stale back to vitality, all that is withholding back to flow, and all that is absent back to presence in your life. I bless you to be free and flowing in your recognition and appreciation of others, mirroring my endless abundance to all who have turned away and forgotten to connect to Source. I bless you with the gift of generosity so that you may be my personal messenger to all, announcing that Divine Source supplies all needs, and that there is no lack for those who recall and connect to their true and divine nature.

And so I decree it in my name, your most Holy Mother-Father God who created you and loves you unconditionally; the love, light, and healing of the Christ; and the power of the Holy Spirit, the breath of life that awakens your generous and gifted Spirit this day, and lives and moves in your being.

Message from Spirit

Open your heart, and there you will discover the gift of humor. Humor temporarily frees you from immersion and enslavement to the soul's struggle and the ego's drama, and elevates you back to the viewpoint of Spirit. Laughter, amusement, chuckles, smiles—all are the many faces and expressions of the gift of humor. Humor restores perspective, returns one's sense of power, rebalances and liberates one from negative and toxic emotions, and elevates one's vibration to detachment and freedom in a moment. It floods the body with healing hormones and brings relief and objectivity to the mind.

The gift of humor is ushered into your heart by the divine muses, the subtle joy guides of creative inspiration and solution in service to God. They are there to remind us that what we laugh at we can overcome. Search deep into your heart to find your gift of humor, especially if it feels lost at the moment. It doesn't go away. It's only been misplaced. Follow the muses and look for your gift in humorous movies, funny books, comedies, jokes, and satires. You can find the gift of humor if you look for it. That is part of the fun of humor. When you look closely enough for it, you find it in everything.

Invocation

By the power of the Holy Mother-Father God, Source of all life, I invoke the muses of humor to stand with me this day, bringing with them the divine gift of laughter and play, delight, and amusement at the way life unfolds before me. I call upon the angels of joy to gift me with mirth to tickle my funny bone, and to raise in me objectivity and detachment of ego so that I am able to see my own silly games as well as those of others, when I pretend to be in control of the Universe while trying to hide my own vulnerability and confusion with little success.

I invite the joy guides of the Universe to tease me today, encouraging me to freely laugh at myself when I am out of control, or feel anxious or fearful so that these shadows quickly disperse by the light of my Spirit. I invoke the gift of humor as I share with others stories of my personal foibles with abandon and affectionate amusement. I invoke my Spirit to bless me with the gift of humor so that I may laugh my way through this day.

Today's Mantra

I am gifted with humor, and I am empowered.

Your Personal Blessing

Today, _____ (your name), I, your ever-loving Holy Mother-Father God, Creator of the Universe, bless your Spirit with the gift of humor and awaken in you the power to laugh easily and readily at everything that unfolds.

Gifts

I invoke my most treasured and divine muse, Thalia, heavenly queen of humor, accompanied by her faithful joy guides, to come to your side this day and fill your thoughts with witty notions, clever ideas, satire, parody, and jokes so that you completely surrender in relaxation to the holy intentions of life and fully experience the peace I bring you. I bless your Spirit with the ability to remain detached and objective, able to witness life's follies and foibles with affection, amusement, and lighthearted acceptance. I bless your Spirit to be aware of the ridiculous posturing of the ego in all, including yourself, and its many silly maneuvers, pretending that it is in control in life.

I bless your Spirit to laugh out loud, with others, at your own mistakes, so that you learn from them without shame, guilt, or embarrassment. I bless your Spirit to see past surface appearances, and recognize and smile at the hidden Spirit in all things, even when the ego attempts to conceal it from you. I bless your day with comedy and entertainment, sprinkled with silly moments, surprising turns, and unexpected twists that cast light on all dark shadows and reveal the truth behind all fear.

I bless your Spirit with a natural ease and glow as you move through the day, free of negative judgment; self-conscious, controlling behavior; and inauthentic expression. I bless your Spirit to be quick to dance and sing throughout the day, filled with the companionship of my many clever muses in heaven, who seek only to delight and uplift your heart in joy. I bless and fill your day with childlike wonder and amazement, thrilling you with funny moments that tickle your Spirit and fill your body with my boundless effervescence and love.

And so I decree it in my name, your most Holy Mother-Father God who created you and loves you unconditionally;

the love, light, and healing of the Christ; and the power of the Holy Spirit, the breath of life that awakens your most gifted and humorous and lighthearted Spirit this day, and lives and moves in your being.

Message from Spirit

Speak from your heart, and share the uplifting and loving force of Spirit with others. Turn a deaf ear and voice to the endless drone and drama of ego, and respond in its place with inspiring and loving messages acknowledging the Holy Spirit within. Affirm the goodness of others and of life, and ensure the positive purpose hidden behind all life experience, waiting to be discovered. Use the gift of inspiration that lies quietly in your heart, and be a messenger of good news and uplifting force. To use the gift of inspiration is to assist others to call their Spirit in.

Invocation

Today, I invoke the power of the Holy Spirit to move through me and use me as a source of inspiration and encouragement to all those whom I touch this day. Let me be the carrier of good news and joyful announcements, reminding people of the many blessings that we are given and share in this life. Use me to cast away the clouds of dreariness, and bring through me the warmth of divine love and healing. I ask all heavenly helpers available to me to empower my words with love and sweetness, lightheartedness and laughter so that when I speak, people open their hearts and hear my good messages. I am present and available to be the messenger of gladness and love that comes from you, Great Creator, this day.

Today's Mantra

I am gifted with inspiration, and I am empowered.

Your Personal Blessing

Today, _____ (your name), I, *your ever-loving Holy Mother-Father God, Creator of the Universe, bless your Spirit with the gift of my presence, the Most Holy Spirit, in your very being, bringing inspiration and encouragement to everything you need and touch.*

I bless your Spirit with profound joy as you sense my presence in your heart and feel it radiating throughout your entire being and into the aura that surrounds your body, encircling you with a blessed glow and attracting light. I bless you with a personal and intimate knowing of my endless love for you this day, clearing from your consciousness all energetic interferences, all subconscious blockages, and outworn negative thought patterns that in the past, kept you from feeling my love and inspiration in your every thought, your every feeling, your every heartbeat.

I bless you with confidence so that as you speak this day, _____ (your name), the words that flow from your lips come directly to you from the heart of me, your Holy Mother-Father God who loves you unconditionally now, forever, and always, beyond any measure you can possibly imagine. I bless you with an endless flow of ingenious ideas, creative solutions, and contagious inventions, attracting to you unlimited enthusiasm and support from others for the gifts of inspiration I bestow upon you this day and every day.

I bless your being with direct contact with me, Source of all life, flowing into your mind and heart, and into your action before you can even think. I give you an open and receptive mind so that you receive all the inspiration I give you to enlighten your brilliant Spirit wherever you go. I bless you with a profound awareness of the endless ways in which every challenge you face can be conquered, every problem you encounter brilliantly solved, every need you have quickly and completely met with the gift of divine inspiration flowing from my angels and helpers into your mind. I give you the inspiration of heaven, as you are my beloved child, my holy treasure whom I love unconditionally and take great joy in showering with my love and blessings.

And so it is decreed in my name, your most Holy Mother-Father God who created you and loves you unconditionally; the love, light, and healing of the Christ; and the power of the Holy Spirit, the breath of life that inspires your most gifted Spirit now and forever.

Message from Spirit

Silence the doubt and suffering of the ego by drawing upon the gift of faith that lies in your heart. Still the mind and feel the force of love and goodness that this Universe has for all. Open your eyes to the beauty around you, in you, in others, in everything. Believe in life. Believe in your Spirit and the Holy Spirit to oversee all. Draw upon the gift of faith to help stop feeling the need for soul and ego to control life. Call upon your faith that is lying in your heart, and let go of the futile notion that all is not unfolding as it should. Call upon the Spirit within to activate your gift of unwavering confidence in life and in the power and force of the Holy Mother-Father God to oversee all. Relax. Allow. Have Faith.

Invocation

By the power of the Holy Mother-Father God, Great Creator and Source of all life, I invoke the Holy Spirit to instill in me this day the gift of faith, giving me unwavering confidence in your omnipotent power and love to oversee my life. I call upon the unseen heavenly forces of protection to help ease my fearful anxiety and rest my troubled mind. Using the gift of faith, I know with absolute certainty that all shall unfold according to your holy plan, and I have no need to fear. I surrender all personal control and worry over to you, Mother-Father God, and draw upon the faith placed in my heart and Spirit to allow me to peacefully await the most beneficial outcomes for all concerned in all matters in my life.

Today's Mantra

I am gifted with faith, and I am empowered.

Your Personal Blessing

Today, _____ (your name), I, your ever-loving Holy Mother-Father God, Creator of the Universe, bless your Spirit with the gift of faith in me to watch over, protect, nurture, guide, and lead you this and every day of your life.

I bless your Spirit with the heavenly support and companionship of dear Brother Thomas, my Apostle, to shine a light on your path every step of the way, _____ (your name), so that you can sense, feel, and trust the presence and power of my love surrounding you, knowing without doubt in your heart and soul that there is never a thing to worry about, as I am with you. I bless your Spirit, my beloved and treasured child, and I delight and take great joy to have you walk in peace and confidence throughout your earthly life, living by your Spirit and with calm in your thoughts.

I bless your endeavors and bring positive fruition to your goals and intentions this day, asking you to be certain of the outcome of success in all that you do. I bless and shower you with affection and approval, as I have created you in perfection. You are guided to be only the best and most authentic you this day, ever faithful that this is all you must be, now and forever. Laugh and dance with the joy that rises in your heart this day, my dear one, faithful to your Spirit and present to my love.

And so it is decreed in my name, your most Holy Mother-Father God who created you and loves you unconditionally; the love, light, and healing of the Christ; and the power of the Holy Spirit, the breath of life that activates your deepest faith in my love and protection, overseeing all in a perfect plan, now and forever.

Message from Spirit

Open your heart to find the gift of beauty lying within. Use this gift to bring more beauty to our holy planet and blessed people. Begin by bringing out your own beauty. Smile and allow the light of the Holy Spirit within to shine through your eyes and out into the world. Bring a neat and fresh appearance to others, free from dreariness and disarray. Place your attention and priority on making your environment, the space that you have been gifted to use, more beautiful.

Arrange, organize, and clean with cheer in your heart, so that the Holy Spirit that resides in you, in others, in all is blessed with a place of beauty and sanctuary to rest this day. Let your words be beautiful and uplifting, free from vulgar expression or curse, and demoralizing messages to others. Let your thoughts be beautiful so that you contemplate the blessings you have been given. Spread the beauty of Spirit wherever you know that all sentient beings will feel your beauty and thus activate it in themselves as a result.

Invocation

Blessed and emboldened by the Holy Spirit in me, I call upon the gift of beauty to grace my life in every way this day. Let me channel this gift through my own being, by bringing forth the beauty of my Spirit to share with the world. Let my smile beautify my face and my eyes twinkle with light as they reflect the beauty that I see and appreciate all around me. I invoke the divine forces of God's holy sister Venus and her heavenly aides to bring out the best and most beautiful effort in me this day, both inside and out. I honor the Holy Spirit that dwells in me, by creating beauty and grace in my home and workplace, through order, light, cleanliness, and simplicity. I speak beautiful words and acknowledge the beauty in others with my words. By the power of the Holy Spirit in me, I contribute beauty to the world with my creations in every way this day.

Today's Mantra

I am gifted with beauty, and I am empowered.

Your Personal Blessing

Today, _____ (your name), I, your ever-loving Holy Mother-Father God, Creator of the Universe, bless your Spirit with the highest gift of beauty, and command it to radiate through your entire being: body, mind, and soul.

I call forward from heaven my most beloved Archangel Jophiel to shower your Spirit with beauty in all forms this day. I bless you with and give you sweet and exotic scented flowers and magnificent trees to shade and scent your way. I give you beautiful winged creatures to lift your Spirit and remind you to soar above the clouds of heavy earthly existence. I give you the companionship and devotion of domestic animals that *love and serve you unconditionally. I bless your Spirit with the beauty of the wind on your face this day, clearing away the fog and confusion of dark and troubling thoughts. I bless your Spirit with the beauty of clear water to wash away the dust and debris of negative patterns that have settled upon your mind and drain away your confidence.*

I bless your Spirit with a clear view of all, free from judgment and condemnation, recognizing the perfect and holy essence in all beings. I bless your Spirit with internal fire to keep you active and energized, and faithful to your goals and intentions. I bless your Spirit as you move day by day, and I make holy the ground under your feet, supporting your path with beauty and comfort. I bless your Spirit with beautiful experiences this day that will enlighten your ego and remove the burdens of your soul.

I bless your Spirit, _____ (your name), to receive the beautiful gifts from all that unfolds, learning from it what is necessary to move forward in higher consciousness so that you bring light and beauty to places where there was once darkness. I bless your Spirit, my most gorgeous and beloved child, whom I created in perfect beauty and light, and in whom I take great delight. I bless your Spirit and celebrate your existence. I am pleased with you in every way and affirm that you are indeed created in my image and likeness, and are therefore a divine and holy and most beautiful presence on earth.

And so it is decreed in my name, your most Holy Mother-Father God who created you and loves you unconditionally; the love, light, and healing of the Christ; and the power of the Holy Spirit, the breath of life that gives you beauty and holds you in my love and protection, now and forever.

Message from Spirit

Open your heart to find the gift of healing lying therein. Have clear awareness and an unwavering gaze to see others in the wholeness, goodness, and light of their Spirit, not in the shadows and fragments of their soul or ego. Use this healing gift to help call these fragments of authentic Self home in others. By the power of the gift of healing, you can restore distorted and unloving percep-tions of self and others to their divine, complete, beauti-ful, authentic nature. Look upon the world with loving eyes and heart, and the healing power within you will flow. Speak to the Spirit within all, not the distorted ego or lost soul, and their light will activate.

Be kind. This is the greatest expression of healing there is. Let the Holy Spirit fill your heart with profound kindness, removing all temptation to judge from the ex-terior, knowing that it is rarely an accurate or true reflec-tion of the person or persons you encounter. Embrace the gift of healing bestowed upon you by the Holy Spirit, and use it freely. In it you possess a great power to help restore others to wholeness.

Invocation

By the power of the Mother-Father God and the Holy Spirit that dwells in me, and with the assistance of

Archangel Raphael, overseer of wholeness, I invoke the gift of healing to activate, amplify, and course through my being this day. I call upon all divine angels and healers in heaven to work though me to call home the holy and authentic Self in me that is complete in every way. I command the ego, soul self, and all lower frequencies interfering with God's wholeness to surrender to the healing power of the Holy Spirit present in this moment. I invoke the Holy Spirit and divine helpers to recall all lost pieces and aspects of Self, reclaim all shattered confidence and denied or unexpressed creativity, and bring forward the divine and unlimited true nature of wellness. In gratitude and joy, I accept and embrace the gift of healing, and let it flow freely through me to all who are in need this day.

Today's Mantra

I am gifted with healing energy, and I am empowered.

Your Personal Blessing

Today, _____ (your name), I, your ever-loving Holy Mother-Father God, Creator of the Universe, Source of all life, bless your Spirit with the highest gift of healing power, overseen by my glorious attendant and servant in the light, Archangel Raphael, instilling in you the ability to call into your being and all beings whom you touch a complete wholeness of Spirit and peace of body, mind, and soul.

I endow you with the ability to calm the emotional waters within, and bring calm and centered peace to the emotional waters of all those who seek peace. I give you the holy *power to quiet the internal winds of mental turmoil, and bring stillness of thought, keen awareness of intuition, and Divine Guidance within. Clarity and deep wisdom command my holy light to radiate throughout your entire being, body, mind, and soul. I bless your Spirit, _____ (your name), and give you the power to ease soul pain and mental patterns of suffering and depression. Wherever you go, you will be mindful of your powerful impact on all, and with the gladness of Spirit channeled to you by Raphael's most radiant vibration, you will be one to instill peace and security where there is drama and fear.*

I give you the assistance of my many angels of light, so that as you summon wholeness and health, they will work for you to gather all lost pieces of Self that have scattered in your earthly soul journey, and return all back to you. I bless you with and give you the most healing vibration of love, instilling your words with the vibration of soothing music to quiet the fragile and tormented soul wounds of those who suffer. I give you the power of healing touch, allowing the Holy Mother's light to arise in your heart and move through your hands to comfort and strengthen and restore others to the wholeness of Spirit within. As my divine child, you are gifted with the power to heal with your presence and return all those who've run from their light to the Holy Mother-Father God who awaits their homecoming.

And so it is decreed in my name, your most Holy Mother-Father God who created you and loves you unconditionally; the love, light, and healing of the Christ; and the power of the Holy Spirit, the breath of life that activates your deepest faith in my love and protection, overseeing all in perfect plan, now and forever.

Message from Spirit

Open your heart to find the gifts of organization and order made available to you. In working with these sister gifts, you are able to center your thoughts and hold your attention on specific desired goals long enough to draw them into your life as manifest reality. Using these gifts allows you to rise out of the random chaos of reactive and unconscious victimhood, and become an effective Master Creator in your human journey. Build your life as you command. By the power of organization and focus, you are able to refuse all distraction of mind and emotion that does not support and build your intention.

You are able to easily steer clear of all that does not strengthen your goal and reinforce its expression. Call upon this gift to hold clear and focused intention for self and others. For self it is felt as creative power. For others it is experienced as leadership and guidance. All thought is destined to reflect in the human experience, for self and others, and those who have the gift of organization and focus create and attract the best and most desirable of reflections. Embrace these sister gifts that are lying in wait in your heart, and use them to move toward mastery in creating your life and leading others.

Invocation

By the power of the Holy Spirit in me, and with the help of the heavenly angels, I invoke the gift of organization to arise in me, to ground, center, and strengthen my life this day. I command all patterns of chaos and self-undoing, both conscious and unconscious, that I carry or that are around me to give way to the higher divine frequencies of peace and organization. I call upon the order of heaven to redirect my life energy and the life patterns of those with whom I interact this day into harmonious flow with the godliness, beauty, empowerment, and mastery of heaven. I release any conscious or unconscious attachments I hold to drama, disorder, confusion, disarray, and destruction, and use the gift of order that I possess to replace these frequencies with clarity, discernment, and precision in my decisions and behaviors, while eliminating all that is unnecessary or distracting to my highest good and authentic nature.

Today's Mantra

I am gifted with order, and I am empowered.

Your Personal Blessing

Today, _____ (your name), I, your everloving Holy Mother-Father God, Creator of the Universe, Source of all life, bless your Spirit with the empowering gift of order, overseen by my glorious attendant and Ascended Master, Serapis Bey, accompanied by his attendant in love, Archangel Raguel, guardians of harmony, order, organization, building, and structure, helpers to those who wish to create and manifest on the physical plane.

I gift your Spirit with clear and grounded thinking so that your intellect supports your Spirit fully to bring your ideas and goals to fruition. I gift your Spirit with the power to communicate with others in a fluent and comprehensible manner, received with understanding and support. I gift your Spirit, _____ (your name), with the ability to share your ideas in a clear and organized fashion so that people to whom you are speaking feel enthused and open to receive them.

I bless and gift your Spirit with the beauty that order brings, eliminating from your thoughts and emotions all that is unnecessary or interruptive to your success. I gift your Spirit with consistency of thought and feeling, allowing only that which fully supports and strengthens your Spirit to flow through you this day. I bless and gift your Spirit, _____ (your name), with beautiful and grounded ideas, and supportive action that brings your goals and intentions to life. I decree that the heavenly forces of order oversee all that comes from your being, removing from the flow of your life any energies that would close your heart.

And so it is decreed in my name, your most Holy Mother-Father God who created you and loves you unconditionally; the love, light, and healing of the Christ; and the power of the Holy Spirit, the breath of life who offers the deepest love and protection for you my holy child, overseeing all in your life as my perfect plan, now and forever.

❧ ✿ ☙

Message from Spirit

Open your heart, and there you will find the spiritual gift of compassion waiting to be expressed. This gift of Spirit bestows in you a deep awareness and sensitivity toward the suffering of others, and activates a desire to reach out immediately in whatever way possible to alleviate or reduce the suffering you encounter as you walk through life. The gift of compassion moves your heart and mind to action.

Rather than look the other way or with a cold heart when you witness the suffering of another, through the divine gift of compassion, you respond to the pain of others with the same tenderness and care as if it were your own or that of one you love deeply, and then do all in your power to help relieve the pain without taking it on yourself. The gift of compassion removes from your heart all inclination to judge, condemn, ignore, or deny the pain of others, replacing these lower, ego-centered distortions with a clear heart and loving action to assist without hesitation. This gift lies in you, waiting to be freed. Reach for it.

Invocation

Holy Mother God, Creator and Source of all life, I invoke your angels and heavenly guardians to awaken in me the powerful gift of compassion, that I may be useful in relieving some of the pain, anger, and judgment of this world this day. I ask the highest heavenly guides available to assist me this day in awakening within me a deeper understanding of all human suffering, and in opening my heart so that all suffering may subside a little this day. I invoke my Higher Self, the Holy Spirit in me, to find compassion for my own suffering and shortcomings as well, so that as I heal, I may be more open, sensitive, and tolerant toward the suffering and struggles of others. I call upon the powers of intuition and insight to help me erase the errors in my own thinking that allow for me to turn my heart away from another or turn negative judgment on myself.

Today's Mantra

I am gifted with compassion, and I am empowered.

Your Personal Blessing

Today, _____ (your name), I, your everloving Holy Mother-Father God, Creator of the Universe, Source of all life, bless your Spirit with the divine gift of compassion.

By the power of this most enlightened gift, your heart opens with love and sensitivity for all creatures on earth this day, allowing you to serve as a force of healing and comfort to your fellow human beings. I invoke the power and love of my most beloved Ascended Master of Compassion, heavenly sister, Quan Yin, to fill your heart with her mercy for the pain and suffering in the world, enabling you to do your utmost to offer relief, even if only with a simple word or gesture of kindness. I bless and gift your Spirit with many opportunities this day to spread love and compassion on my behalf, reaching out to all who are in need, with ease and joy, filling you with more energy and self-love with each benevolent effort you make this day.

I bless and fill your Spirit, _____ (your name), with tenderhearted sweetness, thoughtful consideration, and charity for those in need, such that you do not take on their burdens. I bless and fill your Spirit with the companionship of thousands of angels of mercy, led by Archangel Chamuel, who will work by your side this day, keeping you free of others' pain, sadness, and heavy hearts. I bless and fill your Spirit with the gift of compassion for yourself, as well, filling you with love for your soul's journey as you learn your soul lessons with grace and dignity, and meet your soul challenges with honesty and strength.

And so it is decreed in my name, your most Holy Mother-Father God who created you and loves you unconditionally; the love, light, and healing of the Christ; and the power of the Holy Spirit, the breath of life who instills in you my deepest love and compassion for all creatures on earth, now and always.

Message from Spirit

Open your heart, and there you will discover the gift of service. It waits to be noticed and used in support of the betterment of all people and all of life. It is expressed in both big and small ways. It makes no difference. In the eyes of heaven, all service is a welcome expression of love. Call upon the gift of service to friends and neighbors in doing your part to make the community stronger, better, safer, and more friendly. Call upon the gift of service to bring support and assistance to those with whom you work, making the workplace more grounded, calm, and uplifting. Extend the gift of service to family, caring for children, assisting the elderly, and entertaining and talking with teenagers.

When possible, assist in the schools. Coach. Be available for after-school programs. Volunteer for fund-raisers and tutoring. Offer your gift of service to those who need transportation, an extra hand, a cup of sugar. Offer to serve before being asked. The gift of service makes you available to be asked for help without fear. To serve is to treat others with respect, love, and support in their hour of vulnerability and to do so with gratitude and pleasure. Find the gift of service in your heart. Use it in service to your personal Spirit.

Invocation

Holy Mother-Father God, by the power of the Universe, Source of all Life, I invoke the angel guardians of heaven to activate in me the gift of service. I invite my friends and helpers in Spirit to help me use my gift of service this day to bring relief, assistance, care, and a kind energy to the world. I call upon my Spirit to set aside my ego and serve my fellow humans with courtesy, gratitude, enthusiasm, and respect. Let me be an earth angel and walk today in service to you, my great Creator, and spread your love and healing wherever I go. Open my eyes to see beyond my own needs and recognize where I can render service to another. Open my ears to hear beyond my own mental chatter where my service is needed, and then guide me to help. I ask to be used in service to your holy plan this day, Mother-Father God, and I gratefully await your direction.

Today's Mantra

I am gifted to serve, and I am empowered.

Your Personal Blessing

Today, _____ (your name), I, your ever-loving Holy Mother-Father God, Creator of the Universe, Source of all life, bless your Spirit with the loving gift of service to your fellow human, overseen by my heavenly attendants Archangels Uriel and Aurora.

I bless your Spirit with the ability to intuitively know what others need and to kindly offer your help and guidance.

I bless your Spirit to be present and supportive to the greater good in all situations and assist gladly with a quiet manner, directing people away from drama and toward solution and creative outcomes with your influence. I bless your Spirit with the power to reach out and extend your personal insight and talents to those whom you touch this day, making it easier and more pleasant for each one to get through the day.

I invoke the Spirit of my most blessed son, Master Teacher Jesus, the Christ, to come to expand your heart and mind with his heavenly vibration, so that you know that all you do with love for others, you do in his name, which returns to you a thousandfold in blessings and manna from heaven. I bless and empower your Spirit to serve others this day without the need to attract attention to yourself, letting your actions be reward enough. I direct a thousand angel guardians to walk alongside you, _____ (your name), gifting you with ideas and inspiration on how to quietly serve humanity this day, expanding the circle of love and peace on earth with every act of service you share. I bless and empower your Spirit with the gift of service so that you continue to follow your Holy Spirit's plan to move away from ego and out of soul drama, and return to Source energy, the light of your God, this day.

And so it is decreed in my name, your most Holy Mother-Father God who created you and loves you unconditionally; the love, light, and healing of the Christ; and the power of the Holy Spirit, the breath of life who instills in you a call to quiet service for all creatures on earth, now and always.

Message from Spirit

In the whirl and blur of the anxious world and hurried mind, turn to your heart and find the gift of patience. Draw upon this gift of Spirit to return to flow with the pace of divine timing over human urgency and control. Breathe this gift forward from your heart and allow it to create the space for life to unfold as it will, without fear and struggle. Access the divine gift of patience lying in your heart when your ego feels that it must crowd, force, push, insist, defend, attack, and fight to be seen, to win, or to get results. Patience is the wise old man of spiritual gifts. It does not rush or hurry. It steps back rather than surge ahead. Patience is the act of trusting God's divine plan over your ego's plan or your soul dramas. Patience is not passive. It is a keen gift of awareness that tunes in to divine knowing over personal agenda and assumes nonpersonal awareness over subjective personal reaction. Patience gives people the opportunity to recalibrate to a higher frequency when they falter.

Invocation

Most Holy Mother-Father God, Creator of the Universe, and Source of all Life, I invoke you this day to bestow upon me the most powerful gift of patience. Allow my ego to step back and watch, learn, and support my Spirit to fully trust and allow the Universe to unfold in its own time and in its own way without my interference or interjection. I invoke the teachers in Spirit to restrain my own personal sense of urgency and drama, and fill my being with calm assurance that all things are unfolding in due time and in accordance with God's holy plan and not my own.

Please restrain me from reacting to others with frustration or judgment if they do not behave according to or comply with my grand ego schemes, and give me the patience to allow and forgive all mistakes, errors, and confusion—others' and my own—that tax my personal sense of control or timing. Holy keepers of time, keep me from compressing time in my mind to create tension, stress, and fear, and instead let time stretch to the edges in order for all things to play out in their own natural timing according to your holy plan. I call upon the gift of patience and consciously anchor it firmly in my heart and mind, fueling it with the full and deep breath in my body, and expanding it with every exhale that follows. I am blessed with patience and use it fully this day.

Today's Mantra

I am gifted with patience, and I am empowered.

Your Personal Blessing

I, your most Holy Mother-Father God, Creator of the Universe, and Source of all Life, call forward this day the divine

gift of patience to fill your being, _____
(your name).

I open your heart and bless it with the ability to endure all difficult conditions you meet with confidence in the outcome and tolerance for those who disturb your vibration with their clumsiness and fear. I invoke the divine support of Archangel Gabriel to walk with you through this day, assisting you to peacefully allow for challenging moments and making room for the pace, timing, and flow of life with grace and temperance. I call upon my many angels of patience to keep your holy breath of life steady and your heartbeat calm so that you maintain your internal peace no matter what occurs. I bless your Spirit and free you from anxiety and worry this day, as you surrender fully to the wisdom of my holy plan, which oversees life in all ways.

I bless your Spirit with patience for your and all people's vulnerabilities and weaknesses this day, so you know that, with life, comes human imperfection, which you can accept with humor. I bless your Spirit, _____ (your name), with the gift of others' patience toward you this day as well. Those with whom you engage will be calm and relaxed when interacting with you. Doors will open, and others will patiently wait their turn, allowing you the time and space you need as you move through this day at ease. All will be calm and centered, grounded by the presence of the Holy Spirit in you.

And so it is decreed in my name, your most Holy Mother-Father God who created and loves you unconditionally; the love, light, and healing of the Christ; and the power of the Holy Spirit, the breath of life who instills in you an enduring patience for all creatures on earth, now and always.

Message from Spirit

Quiet your mind and lips for a moment, and you will discover the gift of listening that lies in your heart. Listening is a powerful gift of Spirit, as it allows the one to whom you are listening to be witnessed, feel heard and valued, and better understand his or her own life experience, all of which strengthen the Spirit within. To listen deeply to another, from the heart and with genuine interest, is one of the greatest gifts you can share. To listen is to hold the space and energy for others to safely revisit, relive, and review their life experience from an objective point of view and, perhaps within that experience, discover new insights, fresh perspective, and treasures of understanding that may have been overlooked or bypassed when they were immersed in the experience itself.

To listen gives one a mirror with which to sort out the real from the misperceived, the actual from illusion, the truth from the false. To listen is to allow people to see themselves from a higher perspective. Listening allows the heard the opportunity to emerge from the dark confusion of their ego and soul drama, and see their own experience from the vantage point of Spirit in its place. Listening allows one to feel celebrated as well. It allows one to relive the best of times and infuses joy all over again. To listen to others is to learn from their experience, draw from their gifts, bask in their victories, and grieve with their losses, thus expanding your life experience. Open your heart and quiet your mind. There you will find the gift of listening and all of its treasures for you.

Invocation

By the power of the Holy Mother-Father God, Lord of all life, I invoke the assistance of my heavenly guardians to silence my ego, quiet my heart, and gift me with the power to listen beyond words to the deepest and true meaning behind all communication I am blessed to receive. I ask the healing forces of heaven, in service to our great Creator, to allow me the gift of listening to others, and to help me learn from their experiences and pains, and grow through their joys and breakthroughs. I ask for the help of my divine teachers and guides who, in service to the great Creator, oversee my soul's growth to strengthen my Spirit on earth and to activate in me the power to listen, not just to words, but also to subtle vibration of all that is unspoken, so that I may receive the benefit of the experiences of all and grow my soul with their victories. Most of all, I invoke the Holy Spirit to alert me to its frequency and vibration so that I may listen and follow its force to lead my life at the highest and most beautiful vibration on earth.

Today's Mantra

I am gifted with the ability to listen, and I am empowered.

Your Personal Blessing

Today, _____ *(your name), I, your ever-loving Holy Mother-Father God, Creator of the Universe, Source of all life, bless your Spirit and give you the power to listen to the pulse of the Universe.*

I bring to you the ability to hear beyond the words of others, and understand the deeper meaning and intention behind everything you hear. I bless and gift your Spirit with an ability to encourage others to open their hearts to you, confiding their deepest secrets, needs, and innermost thoughts to you, purging their consciences with light. I bless your Spirit, _____ (your name), with the ability to hear others without absorbing their energy or taking on their troubles, while relieving their burdens. I bless and gift your Spirit with the ability to listen to subtle vibrations as well as spoken word, opening up the power of intuition in your heart to guide your way.

I surround you with the support of my heavenly Ascended Master of divine patience and infinite love Mother Mary, who through you cradles the hearts and Spirits of all who confide in you. I bless and gift your Spirit with the ability to bring forward the truth in those who communicate with you so that you feel safe and fully witnessed in your presence. Through the power of listening to others, you will learn and grow from their experiences, without having to suffer the same trials and tribulations yourself.

I bless and empower your Spirit with the gift of hearing what is essential and true in all situations you face today, even that which is unspoken or unexpressed. I bless your Spirit with the ability to tune in to what is important, while letting the unnecessary or distracting communications go by the wayside, keeping your heart and mind clear and focused on what is important and authentic. This day you will listen to many positive and life-affirming messages, sent by my angels and conveyed to you by surprise through others.

And so it is decreed in my name, your most Holy Mother-Father God who created and loves you unconditionally; the love, light, and healing of the Christ; and the power of the Holy Spirit, the breath of life who instills in you an enduring capacity to listen to your fellow human and to your heart, now and always.

Message from Spirit

Open your heart and tune inside, and there you will discover the glorious gift of music. Music is heaven communicating directly with your Spirit. Feel the music of heaven pulsing through you. Feel the vibration of your personal heart song. Notice its rhythm and tone, the way it gives you energy and feeds your Spirit like nothing else. This beautiful gift from the heavenly Mother-Father God sets your Spirit free. Music carries you beyond the boundaries and limitations of the physical realm and allows you to reach for the edges of your true nature. It gives your Spirit a voice and soothes the wounding of your soul.

Do not miss the gift of music, take it for granted, ignore it, or feel that it has passed you over. All have been given the gift of music to be felt, experienced, and expressed in their own way. For some, this gift is expressed through the speaking voice. For others, it is expressed through the singing voice or through an instrument. And still for others, the gift of music is expressed through their bodies as instruments through dance. Every human being carries in his or her heart the gift of music. Hear the music and free your Spirit.

Invocation

By the power of the most Holy Mother-Father God, Creator of the Universe, and Source of all Life, I invoke the most precious angels above to open my heart and my ears, and shower my being with the gift of God's heavenly music. I ask the Holy Spirit in me to give me my music this day so that I may sing my true heart song out loud. With the divine assistance of the holy angels of music, I tune out ugly vibrations and dissonant noise, and turn my attention fully to the most blessed healing music flowing from heaven to me. I celebrate all earth angels of music as well, who give me their beautiful songs and sounds, and I join in by adding the beauty of my own music to their choir of love.

I call upon the gift of music to assist me in healing old wounds that I carry, erasing grudges and resentments that I feel, helping me move past vague and real doubts and fears of my not being loved, and expanding my heart and mind to feel my Spirit more and more. I call upon the angels of music to move me to dance in the flow of life. I call upon the muses of music to give me new songs and new melodies of joy and inner peace this day.

Today's Mantra

I am gifted with the spirit of music, and I am empowered.

Your Personal Blessing

Today, _____ *(your name), I, your ever-loving Holy Mother-Father God, Creator of the Universe, Source of all life, bless your Spirit and your entire being with the heavenly gift of music, overseen by the most high Ascended Master Hilarion and assisted in love by Archangel Raphael.*

Moving beyond thoughts and words, you will feel Raphael's chorus of angels singing in your heart this day with their celestial sound coursing through your bones and clearing from your being all that is not of your most authentic and Holy Spirit. Inspired by the forces of love and grace arising from the realm of Hilarion, I bless and give your Spirit a personal song in your heart this day, its sweet words filling you with joyful feelings and peace of mind. I send to you the muses, the cosmic helpers of sound, to activate your personal rhythm, reignite your dance, and increase your tempo to that of the most delightful of heaven's energies, allowing your Spirit to move freely this day.

A symphony of pleasures will resound through your ears as you listen to a myriad of musical instruments inspired by the angels and created by your fellow travelers, coming toward you from many surprising directions, sent from heaven to you to lift up your mood and wash clean your heart. I shower you with musical notes from the earth frequencies to the sky and beyond, to ground your body and expand your awareness of love. I give you music both in your heart and all around your being this day, _____ (your name), clearing, with sound and rhythms, all heavy feelings and outgrown soul and ego patterns, so that your personal vibration resonates with that of your heavenly nature as Holy Spirit embodied. I send you my angels to bless you this day with their music, to entertain, clear, heal, and delight you in every way.

And so it is decreed in my name, your most Holy Mother-Father God who created and loves you unconditionally; the love, light, and healing of the Christ; and the power of the Holy Spirit, the breath of life who instills in you the gift of heavenly music, now and always.

Message from Spirit

Breathe in and feel the power of Spirit rising in the center of your heart, activating in you the gift of leadership. To accept this gift, you must not force, command, or coerce, but rather completely surrender. Breathe in and reach for the gift of leadership inside, and let it take over and move you to your highest calling. Embrace this gift of Spirit and overcome the fear and hesitation to follow your heart. Let your Spirit lead and trust it to protect and serve your most authentic Self. This gift of Spirit, you give to yourself. The gift of your most authentic Self is the one you give to the world.

Invocation

Most Holy Mother-Father God, Creator and Source of life, by the power of the Holy Spirit in me, I invoke the gift of free will bestowed upon me to lead my life as I choose. I ask for the power to use my gift of leadership to consciously claim ownership of my own experience. I call upon my Spirit to oversee my free will this day so that I follow my heart, speak my truth, and stand up for my deepest convictions. I accept this most empowering gift to reach for my highest potential by facing my deepest fears. By the power of my leadership to live as I choose and the help of the Holy Spirit in me, I refrain from abandoning myself to temporary approval in pursuit of genuine self-respect. I call on my Spirit to direct my free will to be fully present and faithful to my most authentic Self. I will that thy will be done.

Today's Mantra

I am gifted with the ability to lead, and I am empowered.

Your Personal Blessing

Today, _____ (your name), I, your ever-loving Holy Mother-Father God, Creator of the Universe, Source of all life, bless your Spirit and your entire being with the heavenly gift of free will and leadership, overseen by my most powerful of heavenly leaders, Archangel Michael, supporting your ability to remain true to your authentic Spirit.

I bless you with and give you this day, _____ (your name), the power to overcome all obstacles and ignore all temptations to live other than true to your most holy and divine nature. This day you will stand tall, walk free, and remain unencumbered by the negative influences of others, leading your life as your Spirit chooses, being true to your most holy heart and loving self. I bless you this day with the power to open new doors to your heart's desire, making clear and direct choices that align perfectly with your higher purpose as a Divine Being.

With the protection of most fearless Archangel Michael overseeing your path, you will enter this day overcoming temporary challenges with ease, focusing on the highest goals of Spirit, remaining honest and straightforward with your words and actions, and acting in integrity with your Spirit. I bless you with and give you, _____ (your name), the ability to positively influence others this day, calling forward their integrity and truthfulness, returning to authentic reflection of their true Spirit by your example.

As you move through this day, others will trust your words, respect your decisions, and follow your guidance with confidence that this will serve their highest good. Your inner light will radiate among the crowd, and people will sit up and take notice of your holy presence, showing interest and receptivity to your intentions and goals. Your light will shine out and surround those in darkness and confusion, and your pure and authentic vibration will automatically return them to their true nature.

And so it is decreed in my name, your most Holy Mother-Father God who created and loves you unconditionally; the love, light, and healing of the Christ; and the power of the Holy Spirit, the breath of life who instills in you the gift of divine leadership, now and always.

Message from Spirit

Be still and tune inward, to the heart, and there you will discover the gift of silence. It is not apparent at first. In fact, it is not easy to find this gift under the rumble of thoughts and emotions. At first you may not believe it is there for you. It is. Be still and wait. It is a gift that comes to you. Do not fight the rumble, or try to stop or control it. Just watch the thoughts and feelings pass across your mind, fleeting, temporary, then gone. Be still and wait. Breathe in the stillness. Silence will arrive. Silence is God touching your heart directly.

Invocation

Most Holy Mother-Father God, Creator of the Universe, and Source of all life, I call upon you to bind my fears and anxieties, and quiet the endless noise in my mind so that I may tune in more deeply to the inner peace and healing that comes with the gift of silence. I invoke the guardians of peace to surround me this day and bring with them a soothing balm to my mental agitations and ignorant commentaries, and put them to sleep with my breath. Attune my mind to the sweet gift of silence, and have it hum through my heart and fill my being with light. Give me the ability to witness my thoughts, yet not fight them. Let me observe as my thoughts come and go, as I remain detached and peaceful this day. I am grateful to embrace the holy gift of silence that accompanies my breath as I tune out the world and listen attentively with all my heart to the sound of God's breath flowing in me.

Today's Mantra

I am gifted with silence, and I am empowered.

Your Personal Blessing

Today, _____ (your name), I, your everloving Holy Mother-Father God, Creator of the Universe, Source of all life, bless your Spirit and your entire being with the heavenly gift of silence, so that you cease your thoughts, quiet your emotions, and hear the gentle voice of my love.

I give you this day the absence of distraction and noise, as your prayer without words reaches into the heart of the Universe, where I meet you with unconditional love. In the silence you will hear the hum of life, the love of the subtle realms, connecting directly with the truth of your eternal nature. In the silence I bless you with the symphony of the angels, the choirs of the Seraphim and Cherubim, singing the praises of God, removing from your being all fearful suffering. I give your Spirit this day relief from the endless drone of the controlling ego, and allow you to surrender unto me all that disturbs your sweet and precious Spirit. I invoke the power of the Archangel of Silence to interrupt the forces of thinking and invite the flow of spontaneity, so that you know that I am with you always as you move and breathe this day.

In your silence you will hear the voice of my love for you, brought forward through the most Holy Spirit in heaven, calming the emotional waves coursing through your body, ceasing all mental agitation and commentary, relaxing your Spirit into the embrace of my deep inner peace. I call forward the power of silence to fill your being, _____ (your name), this day, clearing all other voices resonating from your past, leaving only space for me, your most Holy Mother-Father God, to fill you with my eternal and everlasting love. As you sit in silence this day, I hear your deepest prayers and answer them. I command angels of silence to clear the way for you to move fully into the eternal present moment. This day you are gifted with silence. This day you are gifted with peace.

And so it is decreed in my name, your most Holy Mother-Father God who created and loves you unconditionally; the love, light, and healing of the Christ; and the power of the Holy Spirit, the breath of life who instills in you the gift of silence, of peace, now and always.

Message from Spirit

Allow your Spirit to rise above your resistance to living your Spirit, by your search for the gift of courage buried in your heart. Reach deep within and go beyond the obstacles and shadows thrown up by your ego and soul, and there you will be rewarded with the courage to live in this world in truth, Holy Spirit embodied. To receive this gift, you must pass the test of vulnerability. The gift of courage gives your soul the willingness to experience the many necessary little deaths of ego, those of rejection, judgment, humiliation, and mockery of your light by the unconscious among you, while allowing you to face the birthing pains of your authentic Spirit into this world. Seek the gift of courage to allow the false in you to die and your greater truth to be born.

Invocation

Most Holy Mother-Father God and Holy Spirit, Creator of all, Source of life in me and for all, I call upon you this day to awaken and strengthen the gift of courage so lovingly placed in my heart by you so that I may walk steady and remain in true alignment with my Spirit, regardless of disapproval and discouragement, or any other perceived threat that I may receive from others as a consequence of being authentic. I invoke the steadfast and unwavering gift of courage made available to me through your most generous power, to move me today so that I may be the true authority of my life, not enslaved, oppressed, and fearful of those who posture and threaten to take away my power. Give me the courage to speak up without modifying my heart's message. Give me the ability to confront and dismantle what threatens me. Give me the backbone to stand up for what is right and good for me.

Most of all, instill in me the courage to love without fearing vulnerability, loss of control, or abandonment. I invoke you, most Holy Mother-Father God, to encourage me from within so that I may inspire, by my example, the gift of courage in others in my life. I am forever grateful now and always for this most beautiful gift of courage that I now express and share.

Today's Mantra

I am gifted with courage, and I am empowered.

Your Personal Blessing

Today, _____ (your name), I, your ever-loving Holy Mother-Father God, Creator of the Universe, Source of all life, bless your sweet and pure Holy Spirit with the heavenly gift and power of courage to live true to your Divine Self.

I call upon the fearless, loving, divine support of my most devoted Archangel Michael to infuse your Spirit with the heavenly forces of bravery this day, giving you the power to be fully yourself, activating in you a deep and unwavering

*commitment to surrender to your heart. On this day you will
be authentic, outspoken, direct, and genuine with all people
you encounter, hiding nothing that reflects your true and Holy
Spirit. Your words will flow directly from the heart without
hesitation, and your actions will reflect the utmost integrity
and reflection of the Holy Spirit within. You will face challenges and adversity this day, _____ your name),
with grace and bravery, shining your inner light, knowing
that you are never separated from me, the Holy Mother-Father
God, Holy Source of all life.*

*By the power of my blessing upon you, my beloved and
dear child, you are empowered this day with the courage to
be forthright, direct, truthful, and responsible to your heart.
You will immediately ask for what you want and need from
others without hesitation. You will courageously share your
vulnerabilities, reveal your intentions, and ask for and offer
forgiveness where it is warranted, free of false pride or negative soul patterns of fear, which block your loving nature, and
knowing that the power and force of Michael stands behind
and before you, above you and below you, around and within
you, protecting and empowering you in every way. I invoke his
many legions of powerful angels to walk with you this day
and fill your Spirit with the brilliant light of love. I instill in
you a strong adventurous heart to follow your dreams, and to
call forward your intuitive and brave confidence to say yes to
your Spirit and no to your fears.*

*And so it is decreed in my name, your most Holy Mother-
Father God who created and loves you unconditionally; the
love, light, and healing of the Christ; and the power of the
Holy Spirit, the breath of life who instills in you the most holy
gift of courage, now and always.*

Message from Spirit

Open your heart and breathe in the beautiful gift of friendship that sweetens your life. Notice how the worries and concerns of the future or the troubling disturbances of the past disappear in the graceful presence of the friend who loves you. A friend is the one sent by God to recognize, reflect, strengthen, and delight in your Spirit. A friend celebrates your life, accepts you unconditionally, and mirrors the truth of your being. Friendship is the gift that heals your wounds, the source of inspiration when you doubt, your champion when you are stumbling, that offers forgiveness when you err, comforts you when you suffer, and laughs with you throughout it all. Friendship is the gift that makes life meaningful. Recognize and appreciate the gift of friendship so generously being given to you by others. In gratitude give the same gift in return.

Invocation

Most Holy Mother-Father God and Holy Spirit, Creator of all, Source of life in me and for all, I call upon you this day to awaken and strengthen in me the holy gift of friendship that you have so lovingly placed in my life. I invoke the Holy Spirit to have me witness and celebrate the beautiful friends and supporters who have been there for me throughout my life, offering unconditional love, companionship, and acceptance of who I am, both in Spirit and in shadow. Activate in me the ability to be the best friend to others I can be. Give me the power and selflessness to be more loving, kind, generous, entertaining, and patient with people, witnessing the light of Spirit in them and reflecting it back with love and affection. Great and loving Mother-Father God, move me to acknowledge those who have been my friends along the way, taking my attention off of myself today and reaching out to them, thanking them for the riches they have brought and continue to bring to my life.

Let me step away from my own concerns this day and notice how I can be a better friend to another. Make it clear to me this day where I can be more supportive. Guide me to recognize where I can be more caring and helpful. Move me to bring cheer, acknowledgment, celebration, affirmation, and companionship to someone this day. Empower me to be a true and genuine friend to someone in need, sharing the Spirit of life through joy and laughter. I thank you now and always for my gift of friendship, flowing to me and through me, now and always.

Today's Mantra

I am gifted with friendship, and I am empowered.

Your Personal Blessing

Today, _____ (your name), I, your ever-loving Holy Mother-Father God, Creator of the Universe,

Source of all life, bless your sweet and pure Holy Spirit with the heavenly gift of friendship, both on this human plane of existence and from the heavenly realms above.

I bless you this day with beautiful companionship and love, reflecting the hearts and spirits of those who accept and appreciate your perfect and Holy Spirit. As you move through this day, all will express their deep affection for you in every way. Many will reach out to you and offer support, kindness, laughter, assistance, compliments, and endearments, speaking from their hearts and on my behalf, sharing their love for who you are. You will receive surprising gifts as tokens of others' affection for you as a gift from heaven. Opportunities will come your way as a result of others speaking highly of you in the world. My legions of angels will dance all around you this day, making your way light and filled with synchronistic moments of delight, surprise, opening, and joy. Others will extend themselves to be of service, and thank you for being in their lives.

You will radiate, _____ (your name), with wave upon wave of love and endearment for your most Holy and Divine Spirit, celebrated by both heaven and earth. Others will thank you for your friendship and the many blessings your Spirit has brought to their lives. You will be reminded this day of how you've touched the hearts and minds of so many with your love and light, your patience, assistance, ability to listen, creativity, and sweet presence. Life celebrates you this day for being the beautiful friend you have been to so many of my beloved children in life. I bless and honor your Spirit this day for your most precious love and friendship on this earth, for the healing and peace you've offered to so many as a result of your open, generous, and loving heart. The angels on heaven and earth will fill your day with holy moments of gratitude for your presence in our lives.

And so it is decreed in my name, your most Holy Mother-Father God who created and loves you unconditionally; the love, light, and healing of the Christ; and the power of the Holy Spirit, the breath of life who instills in you the most holy gift of friendship, now and always.

Message from Spirit

Open your heart and give voice to your authentic Spirit. Remove all censoring and hesitation that arise from the ego or lurk in fear in your soul, and reach for the gift of truth lying inside, waiting to rise up and pour forth from your lips. Do not fear the gift of authentic expression. It does not require that you be loud or confrontational, aggressive, or argumentative. It does not ask you to fight or struggle or convince anyone of anything. Quite the opposite is true. The gift of authentic expression empowers you to share your truth with the world while not imposing it on another. This gift not only allows for your truth, but also allows for everyone to have a truth, even if it isn't yours.

It is a paradoxical gift, as the more you speak from the heart, the fewer words you actually need to use. When you speak from the heart, the words flow from the Holy Spirit residing in you. They are clear, direct, uncompromised, and loving. The most powerful part of this gift is that people who hear you will believe you. Your words are felt, respected, and honored as true. Furthermore, with the gift of authentic expression, all that you express becomes true. Use the gift of authentic expression, and you only need to say the word, speak from the heart, and it will be so. True words create.

Invocation

Most Holy Mother-Father God and Holy Spirit, Creator of all, Source of life in me and for all, I call upon you this day to awaken and strengthen in me the holy gift of truth that you have so graciously placed in my heart. I invoke the holy power of truth to flow through my heart to inform my thoughts and guide my words so that I may be authentically present and available in all my relationships with other human beings. I invoke the Holy Spirit of truth to reflect throughout my being, not only in the words I choose this day but also in the actions I take. May the truth of the Holy Spirit in me reflect my faithful adherence to living in harmony with my genuine priorities and values so that my actions reflect the most empowered and Divine Being that I am.

I invoke you, most Holy Mother-Father God, to interrupt my thoughts and words whenever I forget and slip backward and begin to express other than the highest truth as I know it. Please intercept and keep me from dishonoring my truth by my passive agreement with dominant negative opinions, and instill in me the strength to speak up, let the voice of my Spirit be heard, and express my true yes and my true no out loud and without fear. I invoke and awaken the power and Spirit of truth to free me from the bondage of my own denial and my attachment to suffering as an abused victim of others. Please let the gift of truth fully embody and activate in me, allowing me to see the truth of any situation before me without bias or filters. Above all, let me live the truth that I am designed to live, as a spiritual being with a mortal body, a child of God. Let me take this truthful remembrance to the entire world, especially to those who have forgotten their truth. I humbly thank you now and always for my gift of truth.

Today's Mantra

I am gifted with truth, and I am empowered.

Your Personal Blessing

Today, _____ (your name), I, your ever-loving Holy Mother-Father God, Creator of the Universe, Source of all life, bless your sweet and pure Holy Spirit with the heavenly gift of truth.

I call forward from heaven, to walk with you this day, my most beloved and blessed Angel of Truth to oversee your way, removing from your path all that does not resonate with your most holy and authentic being. You are free to fearlessly speak the truth of your Spirit this day, allowing your words to bypass your intellect and ego, and arise directly from your heart, sharing only that which reveals and reflects your most holy and divine heavenly Spirit, and communicates to all your love and inner peace.

I bless your eyes to see beyond superficial appearances this day, registering the true reflection of the world before you, understanding without words the deeper intentions and desires of those with whom you interact, informed of all hidden forces and energies, well aware and prepared to make the best and most self-loving decisions. I bless your ears to hear the true meaning behind all words, _____ (your name), so that you unveil secrets, notice which fears and unconscious energies distort the integrity of the moment.

I bless your heart with the power to connect with the true and authentic Spirit of all people, overlooking their shadows and forgiving their mistakes, witnessing and loving the holiness that lies in their hearts. I bless your awareness with the courage and strength to be truthful and open with others this day, allowing them accessibility to your genuine and authentic Self, which in turn will call the same truth from them. I bless your most Holy Spirit with unquestioning acceptance of your true nature as a most holy and beloved child of heaven, free of shame and guilt, forgiven of all past errors, and loved and treasured beyond measure by heaven.

And so it is decreed in my name, your most Holy Mother-Father God who created and loves you unconditionally; the love, light, and healing of the Christ; and the power of the Holy Spirit, the breath of life who instills in you the most holy gift of truth, now and always.

Message from Spirit

Open your heart, and there you will discover the loving gift of nurturing, the healing force and power of the Holy Divine Mother coursing through your being. Allow your heart to soften by drawing in your breath and then exhaling into your generous nature. Notice the gift of nurturing bestowed upon you, and reflect on how you choose to use it. Appreciate your Spirit and watch how it offers support and strength to others. Recognize your personal means of offering comfort and solace, grounding counsel, and practical direction to fellow travelers through life.

Focus on how the gift of nurturing most often comes through you and touches others. Does it come in the way of healing touch? Do you reach out and comfort through holding, cradling, soothing? Does it come in the form of encouraging words? Do you nurture by affirming the worth and value of the one in need? Does it come through in writing? Do you send cards? Loving notes? Do you nurture through the preparation and sharing of delicious and healthy food? Do you nurture those around you by giving flowers? Running errands? Notice how you use your nurturing power to help others grow. You may not see yourself as nurturing, but this gift comes through you in some way. By noticing how you nurture others, you nurture yourself as well.

Invocation

Most Holy Mother-Father God and Holy Spirit, Creator of all, Source of life in me and for all, I call upon you this day to awaken and strengthen in me the holy gift of nurturing that you have so graciously placed in my heart. I invoke you to fully open and activate this gift in me to allow the light and love of your Divine Holy Spirit to flow through me to others. Please allow me to channel my gift of nurturing to soothe the wounded and weary souls who walk before me, and to bring relief and comfort to the stressed and anxious minds that surround me. Allow me to nurture without taking on the pain of others or interfering with their learning experience. Simply direct me to be a light in the dark corners of life, to nurture and grow what is good and worthy in all beings. I am grateful and thank you now and always for endowing me with this beautiful gift.

Today's Mantra

I am gifted with nurturing, and I am empowered.

Your Personal Blessing

Today, _____ (your name), I, your ever-loving Holy Mother-Father God, Creator of the Universe, Source of all life, bless your sweet and pure Holy Spirit with the heavenly gift of nurturing, bringing to this beautiful planet, the loving touch of our most divine and blessed Mother Mary, Queen of the Universe.

I invoke and call forward the support and assistance of my most beloved Archangels Raphael and Jophiel, as well as their divine companion Saint Francis of Assisi, otherwise known as Archangel Ramiel, to work with you this day, to calm, grow, and empower others, nurturing their Spirits and protecting them from the scourge of negativity and self-doubt. I bless your Spirit with the power to channel unto others loving and healing words, so that those who hear your voice remember and believe in their true and most holy nature as divine children of the Universe.

As you speak, your vibration will activate deep self-esteem and personal appreciation of their most Holy Self in all who hear you, cultivating in them the light and purity of their Holy Spirit. I bless all projects you work on this day to become strong, grounded, bold, solid, and successful as your most Holy Spirit grows and strengthens them into fruition. I bless your Spirit this day, _____ (your name), and strengthen in you the gift of nurturing so that the most holy in you is nourished and cultivated into great personal light and power. I nurture your creative efforts this day with the holy forces of love in heaven, so that as you work, all that you envision and desire becomes stronger, more perfect, and available to you.

I bless and cherish your Holy Spirit, beloved child of mine, and nurture you in full and holy expression with every breath you take. As you support the innate goodness in others today, the power and light you share will flow from me to you, without taxing your being in any way. The life force of heaven will flow through your very being and animate all that is beautiful and loving and positive for this planet as it comes into the realm of your personal vibration. As you nurture others with your gift, so, too, does heaven nurture and strengthen you.

And so it is decreed in my name, your most Holy Mother-Father God who created and loves you unconditionally; the love, light, and healing of the Christ; and the power of the Holy Spirit, the breath of life who instills in you the most holy gift of nurturing, now and always.

Message from Spirit

Open your heart, and therein you will uncover the holy gift of teaching, waiting to be witnessed and consciously used by you to enhance, empower, and strengthen the beautiful and creative Spirit within your brothers and sisters of all ages. The gift of teaching comes in many forms. You may express your gift of teaching in the simple act of patiently and lovingly explaining to a child how to do something he or she does not yet know how to do, like tie shoes. Or, your gift may reveal itself in a more complex way, such as helping someone in pain express and release difficult or blocked emotions through your gentle coaching and well-posed questions.

You might teach others to expand their awareness in life through thoughtful conversation, informative ideas, and meaningful dialogue, or you may teach silently, by example, simply doing your best in life with no other reason than to express your excellence. In what we do and how we do it, we teach others all the time. Every day brings you countless opportunities to teach those around you, and you use this gift whether you know it or not. Someone somewhere is watching you today and values what you say and do. When you recognize the gift you possess to teach, to influence, to impress other impressionable human minds with ideas and behaviors springing forth from you, you become a powerful and conscious teacher. The only questions you must answer are, "What are you teaching?" and "Does it empower or disempower the one who is learning from you?"

Invocation

Most Holy Mother-Father God and Holy Spirit, Creator of all, Source of life in me and for all, I call upon you this day to awaken and strengthen in me the holy and blessed gift of teaching. I invoke you to take over my actions and words, and use me as a messenger of your empowerment and love with all people I influence, both knowingly and unknowingly. Guide me this day to speak with the power and love of the Holy Spirit that dwells in me as I interact with people. Use me to guide others toward their own divine light, by being an excellent example of one who lives by the inner light of Spirit.

Let my gift of teaching come through my words this day, encouraging others to look within their heart and Spirit for guidance and direction. Please keep my ego or soul perspective in check, and interrupt me if I am in the process of arrogantly telling others what to do. Please work through me this day to awaken the hearts and minds of those I touch to their own inner wisdom. Let me speak of your empowering ways and share effective tools that bring out the best in others.

I humbly invoke the power of teaching to find me an open vessel to guide and love this day. It is my desire to empower the Spirit in all and teach others to fearlessly shine their light no matter what. I embrace questions, need for assistance by others, and others' confusion this day as my signal to step in and use my gift of teaching to help others learn, by sharing all that I can to the best of my ability. I am grateful for my gift of teaching, and I humbly ask you to strengthen it in me even more this day.

Today's Mantra

I am gifted with the ability to teach, and I am empowered.

Your Personal Blessing

Today, _____ (your name), I, your ever-loving Holy Mother-Father God, Creator of the Universe, Source of all life, bless your sweet, pure, and most Holy Spirit with the heavenly gift of teaching, demonstrated by your words and actions, so that you uplift the hearts and minds of your beloved brothers and sisters to the light.

Walking with the blessed inspiration of Archangel Raphael, who by my wish oversees you this day, your Spirit will open doors to new understanding, engaging conversation, childlike curiosity, and wonder for all of life, exciting a thirst for loving life and learning more with all with whom you engage. As you move through this day, your mind will be expanded with the loving influence of Raphael's heavenly vibration, causing you to intuitively open to new ways to engage in life, inviting your fellow human to join you in seeing the truth of their being, as children of the light.

Your words, inspired by the Holy Spirit within, will flow from your heart, bringing even to you new ideas and divine solutions to present human challenges. Your brilliant actions will inspire and attract others to watch and discover, through you, new and refreshing ways to address and surmount their obstacles. I bless you this day, _____ (your name), with the wisdom of the wise ones in heaven, so that you know when to speak and when to remain silent. I bless you with the necessary language to break through the barriers and walls of ignorance and defended consciousness in others, awakening in them better ways and greater desire to live in peace, activating in their hearts true and deep awareness of their direct connection to love from God as beloved and most holy children of the light of heaven.

I bless you to walk this day with complete satisfaction of heart, mind, and Spirit, knowing that you are indeed living and fulfilling the true and great design of your most holy purpose, simply by shining and sharing your light and love of life, and, by example, teaching others to do the same. You are a blessed and treasured, cherished and loved, holy and pure child of mine, teacher to one and all the power of love to meet all human need. I bless this day as one celebrating in heaven your existence as a divine and enlightened Holy Spirit embodied on earth.

And so it is decreed in my name, your most Holy Mother-Father God who created and loves you unconditionally; the love, light, and healing of the Christ; and the power of the Holy Spirit, the breath of life who instills in you the most holy gift of teaching, now and always.

Message from Spirit

Open your heart and take in a deep breath. Be calm and allow your thoughts to settle down. Exhale. As though watching a movie, notice your fears and worries and the energy they steal from you, leaving you feeling anxious, tired, and drained. Now gather them up and place them in the center of your heart. There, by the gift of peace placed in you by the Holy Spirit, see them ease and dissipate, replaced with a quiet mind and a deep knowing that everything is as it should be, all is well, and you are safe. Embrace the gift of peace, and surrender the internal worry and concern stirred up by your ego to the loving care of the Holy Mother-Father God, Creator of the Universe. Relax. Let go. Allow. Believe. Breathe. Trust. Summon the peace waiting to be felt in your heart by the Holy Spirit to allow your Spirit to be still. If at first your peace feels fragile and weak, ask the Holy Spirit to strengthen it. With practice, peace arrives. Call upon the gift of peace today and give your mind a rest.

Invocation

Most Holy Mother-Father God and Holy Spirit, Creator of all, Source of life me, I call upon you this day to awaken and strengthen in me the holy gift of inner peace. I invoke you to please ease my anxiety and fear, and settle my thoughts and concerns with this most powerful of gifts. Fill my heart and mind with the certain internal knowing that all is in your loving care so that I surrender myself to you fully and relax. Allow your peace to come to me and to help me walk in confidence this day, so that I expect the best of life to greet me, and the best of me to reach out and give back to life. Please allow me to feel peace in all ways, especially in those aspects of my life where I have become discouraged or allowed disappointment to cause me to forget to trust in the light of the Holy Spirit, who is guiding me. I am grateful for my gift of inner peace, and I will spread my peace and calm wherever I go and with whomever I touch this day.

Today's Mantra

I am gifted with inner peace, and I am empowered.

Your Personal Blessing

Today, _____ (your name), I, your everloving Holy Mother-Father God, Creator of the Universe, Source of all life, bless your sweet and pure Holy Spirit with the heavenly gift of inner peace.

I call forward the support and assistance of Archangel Uriel, bringer of peace and angel of optimism and joy, to oversee you this day. With the protection of Uriel, who walks by your side this day, I bless you with the power to allow all uncertainty to pass and to rest your mind in absolute faith that all is unfolding according to my divine plan, all is well, and you and your beloveds are safe. I bless each effort you make this day, guiding you to follow with surety your inner voice as it directs your thoughts and clears your emotions so that you remain intimately connected to Source for all your needs. I bless you with the power to trust without question my power to protect and preserve you this day in the light and love of the Holy Spirit.

By my blessing, _____ (your name), your goals will be met with ease, your intentions fulfilled with grace, and your desires achieved beyond your farthest expectations. I give you the power to live in peace with yourself and others as a Divine Being on earth. Uriel will remove all disturbances of thought and emotion from the past, and block the doubts of others from troubling your heart. By the grace of the Holy Spirit, I keep you free from anxiety this day. You will meet in its place receptivity of heart from others, genuine affection, deep gratitude, playful cooperation, and quiet confidence from all as you extend your peaceful vibration to all. Today your inner peace will calm the energy around you wherever you go. You will live as my divine child, filled with happiness and relaxation, knowing that you are watched over, protected, and loved unconditionally this day.

And so it is decreed in my name, your most Holy Mother-Father God who created and loves you unconditionally; the love, light, and healing of the Christ; and the power of the Holy Spirit, the breath of life who instills in you the most holy gift of inner peace, now and always.

◄▨► ◄▨►

A FINAL MESSAGE
FROM SPIRIT
(AND ME)

I've been guided to add this final blessing to the book, in case there is ever a moment, a situation, or a day when the pages that you open to do not seem quite enough to calm your soul and ego fears and strengthen your Spirit. The following blessing can be said out loud or silently at any time, for any reason, to call in the power of the Mother-Father God and the Holy Spirit within that gives you life to light your way and calm your fears. It is also a great blessing to share with those who have forgotten their Spirit or have become overwhelmed by negative soul and ego patterns, and seem to have lost their way and their inner light. This blessing, channeled from your most loving Creator and Source, carries a particularly powerful, bright, healing vibration, and will immediately change and raise the vibration of those who hear it.

Dear and Beloved Child of Mine,

I bless your most Holy and beautiful Spirit this and every day of your existence. I fill you with grace to bring peace to your heart, guide you through your intuition to see your way, and gift you with the heavenly powers of Spirit to live as the Divine Being you are created to be. May your most cherished Spirit be strengthened and shine bright in the light of my love this day, and may your soul and ego follow your Spirit home to the very the center of my heart. I bless you to walk in the company of angels, and be protected by holy guardians of light and delighted with the loving companionship of joyful humans. I, your Most Holy Mother-Father God, Creator and Source of all life in the Universe, love, treasure, and bless you unconditionally, now and forever.

And so it is by my decree.

Amen and Alleluia.

AFTERWORD

The key to feeling blessed is to acknowledge your blessings every day, out loud and with exuberant gratitude. In this spirit I acknowledge my blessings the minute I receive them and then again each night before I go to sleep. Unless we acknowledge our blessings, it is quite possible that we actually do not recognize and receive them as they fall so sweetly upon us. The best way to acknowledge a blessing is to utter a simple and heartfelt thank-you to both the Universe and the deliverer of the blessing at the same time.

For example, I deeply thank you, my reader, and thank God, my Source and Creator, for giving me, through this book, the privilege, the opportunity to share with you some of the most powerful healing words and prayers in my life. I thank you, my reader, for the trust and time you have given me through your willingness to read this book. I am so grateful for your presence on earth, and I am blessed by your beautiful Spirit, a kindred soul moving with me to the light. I thank you for the gift of your readership and for your willingness to consider the ideas set forth in this book. I also thank the Holy Mother-Father God, Source and Creator of my life and all things in it, for giving me this glorious opportunity to connect with you through this book and for giving me the privilege of sharing this knowledge with you. Our connection is something I could have never created without this blessed assistance from God.

I also thank, with a heart fully open, my publishers, Louise Hay and Reid Tracy from Hay House, for their belief in me and the privilege that they have afforded me to share my work with you. I am deeply grateful for the platform of support that they have offered me in publishing this and many of my other books, and for making them available to so many people around the world. This has been an unbelievable gift from the Universe, made possible through them and all the fabulous support people who work at Hay House to make this and all their beautiful books available to the world. I want to thank my editor, Alexia, who worked so patiently with me to help make this prayer book meaningful. Thank you so very much, Alexia.

I also thank, with all my heart and spirit, the helpers and teachers in my life who have assisted me over the years to recognize and empower my Spirit, have helped enlighten and guide my soul, and have shared invaluable blessings of companionship, friendship, and truthful feedback with me for so many years of my life. I especially want to thank Debra Grace Graves, my dear and beloved friend, who spent many hours helping me write and shape this book to serve others in the simplest, most beneficial way. Debra, your straightforward, "tell it like it is" feedback makes me laugh, pay attention, and learn. I thank my family, Patrick, Sonia, and Sabrina, and all the rest (as there are many) who bless and enrich my life with your glorious and Holy Spirits every day. I cannot believe my good fortune to have you in my life. My gratitude list can truly go on forever, and does.

Afterword

I thank the Holy Mother-Father God for giving me this incredible journey of life. Every day I recognize, more and more what a blessing it is to be alive on this glorious planet at this time.

Thank you, Source. Thank you, Creator. Thank you, life. I am grateful for all the blessings you shower upon me, my family, my friends, my students, my readers, my enemies, and the human race every single day. Thank you. Thank you. Thank you.

— *Sonia*

BONUS CONTENT

Thank you for purchasing *Grace, Guidance, and Gifts* by Sonia Choquette. This product includes a free download! To access this bonus
content, please visit www.hayhouse.com/download and enter
the Product ID and Download Codes as they appear below.

Product ID: 6491
Download Code: ebook

For further assistance, please contact Hay House Customer Care
by phone: US (800) 654-5126 or INTL CC+(760) 431-7695
or visit www.hayhouse.com/contact.php.

Thank you again for your Hay House purchase. Enjoy!

GRACE, GUIDANCE, AND GIFTS Audio Download Track List

1. Grace
2. Guidance
3. Gifts

Running time: 53:55

Caution: This audio program features meditation/visualization exercises that render it inappropriate for use
while driving or operating heavy machinery.

Publisher's note: Hay House products are intended to be powerful, inspirational, and life-changing tools for
personal growth and healing. They are not intended as a substitute for medical care. Please use this audio
program under the supervision of your care provider. Neither the author nor Hay House, Inc., assumes any
responsibility for your improper use of this product.

ABOUT THE AUTHOR

Sonia Choquette is a world-renowned author, storyteller, vibrational healer, and six-sensory spiritual teacher who is in international demand for her guidance, wisdom, and capacity to heal the soul. She is the author of several best-selling books, including *The New York Times* bestseller *The Answer Is Simple . . . Love Yourself, Live Your Spirit!; Ask Your Guides: Connecting to Your Divine Support System; Trust Your Vibes: Secret Tools for Six-Sensory Living;* and *Soul Lessons and Soul Purpose: A Channeled Guide to Why You Are Here*—plus numerous audio programs and card decks.

Sonia was educated at the University of Denver and the Sorbonne in Paris, and holds a Ph.D. in metaphysics from the American Institute of Holistic Theology. She resides with her family in Chicago.

Website: **www.soniachoquette.com**

Hay House Titles of Related Interest

We hope you enjoyed this Hay House book. If you'd like to receive our online catalog featuring additional information on Hay House books and products, or if you'd like to find out more about the Hay Foundation, please contact:

Hay House, Inc., P.O. Box 5100, Carlsbad, CA 92018-5100
(760) 431-7695 or (800) 654-5126
(760) 431-6948 (fax) or (800) 650-5115 (fax)
www.hayhouse.com® • www.hayfoundation.org

Published in Australia by: Hay House Australia Pty. Ltd.,
18/36 Ralph St., Alexandria NSW 2015
Phone: 612-9669-4299 • *Fax:* 612-9669-4144
www.hayhouse.com.au

Published in the United Kingdom by: Hay House UK, Ltd.,
The Sixth Floor, Watson House, 54 Baker Street, London W1U 7BU
Phone: +44 (0)20 3927 7290 • *Fax:* +44 (0)20 3927 7291
www.hayhouse.co.uk

Published in India by: Hay House Publishers India,
Muskaan Complex, Plot No. 3, B-2, Vasant Kunj, New Delhi 110 070
Phone: 91-11-4176-1620 • *Fax:* 91-11-4176-1630
www.hayhouse.co.in

Access New Knowledge.
Anytime. Anywhere.

Learn and evolve at your own pace
with the world's leading experts.

www.hayhouseU.com

Printed in the United States
By Bookmasters